Big Green Egg Cookbook for Beginners

More Than 100 R Fresh and Tasty Barbecue Recipes to Grill, Smoke, Bake & Roast with Your Ceramic Grill

Soard Fobithe

© Copyright 2021 Soard Fobithe- All Rights Reserved.

In no way is it legal to reproduce, duplicate, or transmit any part of this document by either electronic means or in printed format. Recording of this publication is strictly prohibited, and any storage of this material is not allowed unless with written permission from the publisher. All rights reserved.

The information provided herein is stated to be truthful and consistent, in that any liability, regarding inattention or otherwise, by any usage or abuse of any policies, processes, or directions contained within is the solitary and complete responsibility of the recipient reader. Under no circumstances will any legal liability or blame be held against the publisher for any reparation, damages, or monetary loss due to the information herein, either directly or indirectly.

Respective authors own all copyrights not held by the publisher.

Legal Notice:

This book is copyright protected. This is only for personal use. You cannot amend, distribute, sell, use, quote or paraphrase any part of the content within this book without the consent of the author or copyright owner. Legal action will be pursued if this is breached.

Disclaimer Notice:

Please note the information contained within this document is for educational and entertainment purposes only. Every attempt has been made to provide accurate, up-to-date and reliable, complete information. No warranties of any kind are expressed or implied. Readers acknowledge that the author is not engaging in the rendering of legal, financial, medical or professional advice.

By reading this document, the reader agrees that under no circumstances are we responsible for any losses, direct or indirect, which are incurred as a result of the use of information contained within this document, including, but not limited to, errors, omissions, or inaccuracies.

Table of Contents

Introduction 8
Chapter 1: Beef 9
    Steak Hand Pies 9
    Beef Kebabs 11
    Ribeye Steaks 12
    Loaded Burger 13
    Bolognese 14
    Sloppy Joes 15
    Beef Bourguignonne 16
    Barbecued Baby Back Rib Hoagie Rolls 18
Chapter 2: Pork 19
    Pork Kebabs With Raisin Brown Butter And Toasted Peauts 19
    Chilli-Rubbed Pork Pork Chops 21
    Pork Meatballs 22
    Bacon-Wrapped Pork Wings 24
    Cuban Pork (Lechon Asado) 25
    Spanish Pork Tenderloins 26
    Christmas Gingersnap Ham 27
    Cedar Plank Pork Tenderloin 28
    Bone-in Loin Roast 29
    Chinese BBQ Pork 30
    Prime Rib Roast 31
    New York Style Pastrami 32
    Perfectly Smoked Texas Style Brisket 33
    Rouladen 34

  Holiday Sirloin Roast 35

Chapter 3: Lamb **36**

  Rack Of Lamb With Spicy Tzatziki 36

  Grilled Lamb Chops 37

  Leg Of Lamb Ina Rosemary And Lemon Marinade 38

  Greek Lamb Burgers With Spicy Tzatziki 39

  Herb-Crusted Grilled Leg Of Lamb 40

Chapter 4: Poultry **41**

  Southern-Style Grilled Chicken Wings 41

  Chicken all'Arrabbiata 42

  Green Curry Chicken 43

  Rotisserie Chicken 44

  Chicken Cacciatore 45

  Braised Chicken Thighs with Mushrooms 46

  Green Chile Chicken Chili 47

  Glazed And Grilled Sweet Asian Chicken 48

  Chicken Tacos 49

  Turkey Bacon Dogs 50

  Mexican-Style Turkey Burgers 51

  Turkey Shepherd's Pie 52

Chapter 5: Fish **53**

  Grouper With Tomato-Basil Sauce 53

  Southern Catfish With Homemade Salsa 54

  Grilled Tuna With Chili Orange Marinade 55

  Spicy scallops In Coconut milk 56

  Pinot Grigio wine large oysters 57

  Foil Packet Fish Filets 58

Cedar Plank Salmon 59

Greek Sea Bass 60

Grilled Whole Trout 61

Lemon Bed Cod 62

Grilled Tilapia "Ceviche" 63

Grilled shrimp 64

Chapter 6: Vegetables 65

Mexican Cobb Salad 65

Asian-Style Asparagus 66

Garlic Green Beans 67

Chapter 7: Appetizers 68

Bacon Mac And Cheese 68

Italian-Style Blue Cheese Stuffed Portabella Mushrooms 69

Garlic Toast 70

Chapter 8: Side & Salads 71

Bacon Wrapped Pineapple 71

Baba Ganoush 72

Cowboy Caviar 73

Alligator Egg s 74

Grilled Lemon Garlic Zucchini 75

Broiled Tomatoes and Parmesan 76

Grilled Cabbage with Champagne Vinaigrette 77

Chapter 9: Desserts 78

S'mores Ina Sugar Cone 78

Chocolate Chip Cookie Peanut Butter Cup S'Mores 79

Apple Pizza 80

Grilled Pineapple Sundaes 81

Grilled Coconut And Rum French Toast 82

Fresh Peach Crisp 83

Banana Boats 84

Grilled Plums with Honey and Ricotta 85

Pineapple Upside-Down Cake 86

Chapter 10: Pizza and Burgers 88

Italian Ham Pizza 88

Buffalo Chicken Pizza 89

Classic Meat Lovers Pizza 90

Chicken Bacon Artichoke Pizza 91

Basic Pizza Sauce 92

Garlic Clam Pizza 93

Prosciutto Cheese Dogs 94

Jalapeno And Cherry Cola Glazed Ham Steaks 95

Quesadilla Burger 96

Breakfast Burger 97

Classic American Burger 98

Chicken Keema Burgers 99

The Crowned Jewels Burger 100

The Best Turkey Burger Ever 101

Oahu Burger 102

"The Masterpiece" 103

Ham And Cheese Panini 104

Chapter 11: Rubs, Marinades, and Sauces 105

Classic American Brown Sugar Rub 105

English Pub Rub 106

Berbere Spice Mix 107

Asian Rub 108

Adobo Rub 109

Habanero Rub 110

Chile Rub 111

Carne Asada Rub 112

Country Style Rub 113

Mediterranean Spice Rub 114

Chapter 12: Game 115

Venison fillets 115

Saddle Of Hare With Parsnips, Cabbage, And Apple 116

Asian-Style Wild Boar Ribs 117

Conclusion 118

Introduction

If you're an EGG head who wants to test the highest potential of your Big Green Egg, this cookbook is for you, too! This cookbook contains many cooking tips. It is filled not only filled with 100 recipes but also with best practices, secrets and EGG expert advice on how to use the Big Green Egg. It has instructions that are detailed, with mouth-watering pictures that will empower you to start grilling right away.

The Unofficial Big Green Egg Cookbook will bring out the possibilities of cooking, baking, grilling, stewing, and smoking your favorite recipes. From delicious appetizers, delicious mutton kebabs, corn and vegetables, steak. Want to cook something for your vegetarian friends? Want to show off the juiciest pulled pork you've ever tasted? We have everything that will bring out the celebrity chef in you.

With this cookbook, there's no need to worry about what to cook when you have a surprise guests. Just open up the cookbook and choose any exciting recipes that you want to showcase.

Chapter 1: Beef

Steak Hand Pies

Cook Time: 30 minutes
Servings: 8

Ingredients:

- New York strip steaks (2-lbs, 0.9-kgs)
- Butter
- Salt and freshly ground black pepper
- 1 medium-size carrot, diced
- 1 yellow onion, peeled and diced
- 1 medium-size potato, peeled and diced
- Water, divided -3/4 cup
- Worcestershire sauce 3 tablespoons
- All-purpose flour -1 tablespoon
- Fresh parsley, chopped -1/4 cup
- 1 medium-size egg, beaten
- Olive oil -2 tablespoons
- 1 pie crust dough
- Tomato ketchup -1/2 cup
- Barbecue rub of choice -1 tablespoon
- Worcestershire sauce -1 tablespoon

Method:

1. Add a knob of butter to the hot skillet, and melt.
2. Season the strip steaks before adding to the hot skillet and cooking until gently browned on both sides. Remove from the skillet and set aside.
3. Add the carrot along with the onions, and potatoes to the skillet and fry for 5 minutes.
4. Pour 1/4 cup of water followed by the Worcestershire sauce into the skillet, and stir while scraping up any browned bits from the bottom of the skillet. Bring the mixture to simmer.
5. Meanwhile, cut the steak into cubes.
6. Stir the flour into the veggie mixture until entirely combined.
7. Add the cubes of meat along with the remaining 1/2 cup of water.
8. Stir in the chopped parsley and continue to cook for 2-3 minutes.
9. Turn the heat off and set aside to cool.
10. Roll the pie crust out and with a circular pastry cutter, cut out eight, 6-ins (15-cms) circular shapes.

11. Evenly divide the meat mixture between the circles of pastry, spoon into the center of the pastry, and fold the pastry into half-moon shapes.
12. Crimp the pastry edges to seal and brush the surface with lightly beaten egg .
13. Using a sharp knife make a few small slits in the top of each pie, to allow any steam to escape.
14. Bake the pies in an oven set at 370°F (190°C) until golden. Set aside to rest for several minutes before serving.
15. For the sauce: In a bowl, combine the ketchup with the barbecue rub and Worcestershire sauce, stirring to combine.
16. Serve the sauce along with the hand pies.

Beef Kebabs

Cook Time: 24 hours 20 minutes
Servings: 4-5

Ingredients:

- Beef sirloin, cubed(2-lbs,0.9-kgs)
- Olive oil -1/2 cup
- White vinegar -1 tablespoon
- Cumin -1 teaspoon
- Coriander -1/2 teaspoon
- Paprika -1/2 teaspoon
- Garlic, peeled and minced
- Nonstick cooking spray
- Pita bread, to serve

Method:

1. One day prior to grilling, prepare the marinade. In a bowl, combine the oil with the vinegar, cumin, coriander, paprika, and garlic.
2. Transfer the marinade to a ziplock bag and add the cubes of beef. Place in the fridge overnight.
3. When you are ready to grill, remove from the fridge and thread onto skewers. You will need to spray the skewers with nonstick cooking oil before threading.
4. Grill for 5-7 minutes, on each side, until cooked to your preferred doneness.
5. Serve with pita bread.
6. Enjoy!

Ribeye Steaks

Cook Time: 20 minutes
Servings: 2

Ingredients:

- 2 ribeye steaks
- Soy sauce
- Worcestershire sauce
- Steak rub, of choice
- Butter, melted -6 tablespoons
- 1 garlic clove, peeled, minced
- Fresh thyme -1 teaspoon
- 1 onion, peeled, finely sliced

Method:

1. Season the steaks with a drizzle of soy and Worcestershire sauce.
2. Scatter the steak rub over the steaks, and rub it all over, and into the meat. Allow to rest while you preheat the EGG.
3. In a bowl, combine the butter with the garlic and thyme.
4. Place the steaks directly on the grill. Close the EGG'S lid and cook for a couple of minutes.
5. Open the EGG approximately 1-ins (2.-cns) wide to allow some heat to escape. Next, open completely. Turn the steaks over. Replace the lid, and cook for an additional 2 minutes.
6. Once again, open the EGG approximately 1-ins (2.-cns) wide. Next, open completely wide and turn the steaks over once again.
7. Spoon the butter mixture over the steaks.
8. Close the EGG lid, along with the bottom vent and finally add the damper top.
9. For medium to rare steaks, keep the lid closed for a few minutes. Alternatively, for well done, keep it closed for 5-6 minutes.
10. Remove the steaks, set aside to rest and slice.

Loaded Burger

Cook Time: 2 hours 15 minutes
Servings: 8

Ingredients:

- Ground beef (2-lb, 0.9-kgs)
- Worcestershire sauce -1 tablespoon
- Beef seasoning, of choice -2 tablespoons
- 8 burger buns, split
- 8 slices of Cheddar cheese
- Lettuce, shredded, to serve
- Tomato, sliced, to serve
- Red onion, peeled and sliced, to serve

Method:

1. In a bowl, combine the ground beef with the Worcestershire sauce and beef seasoning. Using clean hands form the mixture into 8 hamburger patties.
2. Arrange the patties on aluminum foil and smoke for 2 hours.
3. Remove the burgers from the grill and place on the bottom half of the buns.
4. Top with a slice of cheese, shredded lettuce, slices of tomato and raw red onion rings.

Bolognese

Cook Time: 1½ hours
Servings: 6

Ingredients:

- 2 lbs ground beef
- 4 oz bacon, diced
- 1 cup milk
- 2 cloves garlic
- 1 stalk celery
- 1 carrot
- 1 small onion
- 2 cups chicken broth
- 1 cup red wine
- 1/4 cup tomato paste
- 1 tsp Italian seasoning

Method:

1. In the bowl of a food processor, combine celery, carrot, onion, and garlic and pulse until finely chopped.
2. Preheat the EGG to 300°F.
3. Place the bacon in a cold Dutch oven and begin heating on the stove over medium heat.
4. Cook the bacon until it is crisp and the fat is rendered.
5. Remove all but 2 Tablespoon of the fat.
6. Add ground beef and cook until brown.
7. Add chopped vegetables and cook for 5 minutes.
8. Add tomato paste and cook for an additional 2 minutes.
9. Add milk and stir. Allow the liquid to evaporate until the milk solids are left behind.
10. Add wine, chicken broth, and Italian seasoning.
11. Cover the Dutch oven and transfer it to the EGG. Allow the sauce to cook for 1 hour before serving over pasta.

Sloppy Joes

Cook Time: 30-40 minutes

Servings: 8

Ingredients:

- 1 lb ground beef
- 1/4 cup onion, finely chopped
- 1/4 cup bell pepper, finely chopped
- 1 clove garlic, finely chopped
- 1/2 cup tomato sauce
- 1/4 cup ketchup
- 2 tablespoons brown sugar
- 1 tablespoon brown mustard
- Salt & Pepper

Method:

1. Preheat the EGG to 400°F with the Dutch oven on the grid.
2. Place all ingredients in the Dutch oven and stir.
3. Cover the Dutch oven and lower the dome for 30-40 minutes or until the beef is cooked through.
4. Serve on hamburger buns.

Beef Bourguignonne

Cook Time: 1 hours 15 minutes
Servings: 6

Ingredients:

- 2½ lbs beef chuck roast, cut into 1 inch cubes
- 1 lb carrots, cut into 1 inch chunks
- 1 lb fresh mushrooms, thickly sliced
- 8 oz bacon, diced
- 1 tsp fresh thyme
- 2 cloves garlic, minced
- 1 onion, sliced
- 2 cups beef broth
- 1/2 cup sherry
- 1/4 cup flour
- 2 tablespoons olive oil
- 1 tablespoon tomato paste
- 1 bottle dry red wine
- Salt & Pepper

Method:

1. Preheat the EGG to 450°F.
2. Place bacon in a cold Dutch oven and place on the grid with the dome closed for 10 minutes or until the bacon is crisp.
3. Drain the bacon on paper towels.
4. Pat the pieces of chuck roast with paper towels to dry and season with salt and pepper.
5. In the hot bacon fat, begin browning the chuck roast in batches, setting each browned back aside.
6. Drain all fat but 2 Tablespoon from the Dutch oven, but reserve it.
7. Add mushrooms and do not move for 5 minutes until they begin to brown. Remove and set aside.
8. Add 2 Tablespoon olive oil to the Dutch oven along with 2 Tablespoon of the reserved fat, the carrots, and the sliced onions. Cook until they begin to soften, about 5 minutes.
9. Add tomato paste and cook 1 minute more.
10. Add flour to the pot and cook for 2 minutes.
11. Add back the beef, bacon, and mushrooms and pour in red wine and beef broth.
12. Add thyme and season with salt and pepper.

13. Cover the Dutch oven, reduce the heat in the EGG to 250°F, and lower the dome for 1 hour.
14. Serve the Beef Bourguignon with crusty bread.

Barbecued Baby Back Rib Hoagie Rolls

Cook Time: 18 hours 10 minutes
Servings: 4

Ingredients:

- 3-4 racks baby back ribs, membranes removed
- Sea salt
- Freshly ground black pepper
- Barbecue sauce, of choice -1 cup
- 4 hoagie bread rolls, split
- 1 large jar of dilled pickles, sliced
- 1 onion, peeled, finely sliced

Method:

1. Season the baby back ribs liberally with sea salt and black pepper.
2. Place the ribs directly on the grill, meat side facing you and cook for 2 hours. Turn the ribs over and grill for 1 hour.
3. Remove from the grill and turn over, so they rest bone-side facing up on a cutting board.
4. With a sharp kitchen knife, cut down the center of each bone, and using clean fingers, carefully remove the bones.
5. Turn the baby back ribs over, and brush with around half of the barbecue sauce.
6. Return the ribs to the grill and grill for between 5 -10 minutes; this will help to set the sauce.
7. Remove from the grill and put to one side.
8. Next, cut the ribs, so they are the same length as the hoagie rolls.
9. Split the rolls and place the ribs on the bottom half of the hoagie.
10. Top with sliced dill pickles, onions and a spoonful of barbecue sauce.
11. Add the top of the hoagie roll to form a hoagie.
12. Enjoy!

Chapter 2: Pork

Pork Kebabs With Raisin Brown Butter And Toasted Peauts

Cook Time: 45 minutes

Servings: 4-8

Ingredients:

- 8 whole pork chops, diced (2-lbs, 0.9-kgs each)
- Sea salt -2 teaspoons
- Olive oil -2 tablespoons
- Unsalted butter -1/2 cup
- Extra-virgin olive oil -1/2 cup
- 4 garlic cloves, peeled, thinly sliced
- Sea salt
- Grated lemon zest -2 teaspoons
- Freshly squeezed lemon juice -2 tablespoons
- Currants -2 tablespoons
- Capers -2 tablespoons
- Toasted pine nuts -2/3 cup
- Parsley, chopped, to garnish

Method:

1. In a bowl, combine the pork with the sea salt and place in the refrigerator overnight.
2. Approximately 1 hour before you begin cooking remove the pork from the refrigerator.
3. Toss the pork with the olive oil.
4. Thread equal amounts of the cubed pork onto the prepared skewers.
5. For the butter sauce: In a large pan set over medium-low heat, heat the butter until it begins to brown and emit a nutty fragrance, for approximately 4-5 minutes.
6. Add the olive oil, followed by the garlic and a pinch of sea salt and cook for 60 seconds.
7. Stir in the lemon zest together with the freshly squeezed lemon juice, currants and capers and cook for a couple of minutes until the sauce begins to reduce.
8. Fold in the pinenuts and set aside while the pork cooks.
9. Over high heat, place the pork skewers directly on the grill and grill on both sides for 1 minute, until seared.

10. Turn the heat down to 300°F (148°C) and continue grilling for 8-10 minutes, until the meat is cooked through.
11. Set the meat skewers aside to rest for 5 minutes.
12. Drizzle the butter sauce over the pork, garnish with parsley and serve with rice or couscous.

Chilli-Rubbed Pork Pork Chops

Cook Time: 2 hours 15 minutes
Servings: 4

Ingredients:

- 4 boneless, skinless sirloin pork chops, 1/2-ins (1.54-cms) thick
- 3 jalapeno peppers, seeded and finely minced
- Sesame oil -2 tablespoons
- Soy sauce -2 tablespoons
- Sugar -1/8 teaspoon
- 2 garlic cloves, peeled, crushed
- Ground cumin -1 tablespoon
- Red pepper flakes -1 teaspoon
- Freshly squeezed lime juice -1/2 cup
- Salt -1/2 teaspoon
- Freshly ground black pepper -1/4 teaspoon

Method:

1. For the rub: In a bowl, stir the jalapeno with the sesame oil, soy sauce, and sugar.
2. Wearing disposable kitchen gloves, rub the mixture all over the pork chops.
3. Arrange the chops in a single layer in a shallow dish.
4. In a cup, stir the marinade ingredients together (garlic, cumin, red pepper flakes, lime juice, salt, and pepper).
5. Pour the marinade over the pork chops and put to one side for between 20-30 minutes.
6. Remove the pork from the marinade, discarding any excess marinade.
7. Grill the chops, flipping over once and cook to a medium level of doneness. This will take between 3-4 minutes on each side, or until an internal meat thermometer registers 145°F (63°C).
8. Set aside to rest for a few minutes before serving.

Pork Meatballs

Cook Time: 2 hours 5 minutes
Servings: 8

Ingredients:

- Ground pork (1-lbs, 0.45-kgs)
- 2 sweet potatoes
- 1 large-size egg
- Parmesan cheese, shredded -3/4 cup
- Seasoned breadcrumbs -1/3 cup
- Fresh parsley, chopped -1/4 cup
- Dried sage, rubbed -1 tablespoon
- Red pepper flakes -2 teaspoons
- Salt, divided -1½ teaspoons
- Vegetable oil, divided -1/4 cup
- Half and half -1½ cups
- Milk -3 4 cup
- Butter -4 tablespoons
- 1/2 sweet onion, peeled, diced
- 3 cloves of garlic, peeled, minced
- Flour -1 tablespoon
- Black pepper -3/4 teaspoon
- Ground nutmeg -1/8 teaspoon

Method:

1. Using a cooking grid, bake the sweet potatoes for between 50-60 minutes, until fork tender.
2. In the meantime, in a bowl combine the pork with the egg , 1/2 cup of Parmesan cheese, breadcrumbs, parsley, sage, pepper flakes, and 1/2 teaspoon of salt.
3. Using clean hands, form the mixture into golf ball size meatballs. Arrange the meatballs on a platter.
4. In a cast iron griddle, warm 2 tablespoons of oil and in a single layer, add the meatballs, and cook for 10-12 minutes, until browned all over.
5. Transfer the meatballs to a kitchen paper towel-lined platter. Cover, keep warm and put to one side.
6. Scoop the potato flesh from the sweet potatoes and add to a food processor and on pulse, process 2-3 times.
7. Gradually add the half and half along with the milk, processing until silky smooth. Set to one side.
8. Using kitchen paper towel wipe out the iron griddle and return it to the EGG at 350°F (177°C). Add the butter along with 2 tablespoons of oil to the griddle and warm.

9. Add the onion along with the garlic and allow to cook until the onion is fork tender, for approximately 5 minutes.
10. Add the flour and cook for 60 seconds.
11. Add in the sweet potato mixture along with the black pepper, nutmeg and 1 teaspoon of salt, and cook for 3-4 minutes, until heated through and thickened. If the sauce becomes too thick, you may need to add additional milk.
12. Finally, while stirring, add 1/4 cup of cheese and cook until evenly heated.
13. Garnish with parsley and enjoy.

Bacon-Wrapped Pork Wings

Cook Time: 2 hours 5 minutes
Servings: 12

Ingredients:

- 4 pork chops, 1-ins (2.54-cms)
- 12 rashers medium-sliced bacon
- Barbecue rub, store-bought
- Barbecue sauce, store-bought

Method:

1. Cut the chops into three strips.
2. Wrap the wings, by overlapping the bacon on one end of a strip of pork, before wrapping it up and around in a candy-cane like fashion.
3. Using a cocktail stick, secure the bacon at the top.
4. Using the rub, season the bacon-wrapped wings.
5. Arrange the wings directly on the grid and cook for 1½ hours, until the bacon is cooked through.
6. Serve the wings hot with BBQ sauce.

Cuban Pork (Lechon Asado)

Cook Time: 10-12 hours
Servings: a small army

Ingredients:

- 1 (7-9 lb) pork shoulder
- 1 recipe Cuban Mojo

Method:

1. Score the skin and fat on the pork shoulder by cutting in one direction, then the other to form cross hatches.
2. Pour Cuban Mojo over the pork shoulder, cover, and refrigerate at least four hours, preferably overnight, turning once.
3. Remove the pork from the marinade 30 minutes before cooking.
4. Preheat the EGG to 255°F, placing the EGG convtor and grid inside.
5. Place the pork shoulder on the grid and close the dome. The EGG is designed to maintain this temperature for up to 18 hours.
6. After 10 hours, check the internal temperature of the pork. Remove the roast when it reads 200°F
7. Carefully remove the pork shoulder from the EGG and allow it to rest 30 minutes before slicing/pulling it apart.

Spanish Pork Tenderloins

Cook Time: 15 minutes
Servings: 6-8

Ingredients:

- 1 pound pork tenderloin
- 2 tsp olive oil
- 3/4 tsp smoked sweet paprika (pimenton)
- 1/2 tsp garlic powder
- 1/4 tsp salt
- 1/4 tsp ground cumin
- 1 cup Romesco Sauce

Method:

1. In a blender, combine all ingredients and blend until smooth. Set aside. The sauce can be made up to 3 days in advance.
2. Combine rub ingredients.
3. Brush tenderloins with olive oil and sprinkle liberally with the rub. Set aside.
4. Preheat the EGG to 450°F.
5. Place the tenderloins on the grid and close the dome for 10 minutes.
6. Flip the tenderloins and cook another 10 minutes or until the internal temperature reaches 150°F.
7. Remove from the EGG and allow to rest for 10 minutes before slicing and serving with the Romesco sauce.

Christmas Gingersnap Ham

Cook Time: 1-1½ hours

Servings: 15-18

Ingredients:

- 1 (8-10 pound) spiral sliced ham
- 2 cups gingersnap cookies, crushed
- 1/4 cup brown mustard

Method:

1. Remove the ham from its wrapper, thoroughly rinse it and pat it dry.
2. Place the ham in a heat-proof roasting pan.
3. Brush the outside liberally with mustard.
4. Press the gingersnap cookies into the mustard coating.
5. Preheat the EGG to 350°F with the convEGGtor® and grid in place.
6. Place the ham inside EGG and close the dome for 1 to 1½ hours.
7. Allow the ham to rest for 20 minutes before carving and serving.

Cedar Plank Pork Tenderloin

Cook Time: 15-20 minutes
Servings: 6-8

Ingredients:

- 2 pork tenderloins
- 1 cup Basic Steak Marinade (not just for steaks!)
- 2 cedar planks (Be sure they are untreated cedar)

Method:

1. Place the pork tenderloins and Basic Steak Marinade in a zip top bag for 30 minutes.
2. Preheat the EGG to 425°F.
3. Place the cedar planks directly on the grid and close the dome for 3 minutes.
4. Turn the planks and place the tenderloins directly on the heated planks.
5. Close the dome for 10 minutes.
6. Turn the tenderloins once and close the dome for another 5-10 minutes or until the internal temperature reaches 155°F.
7. Remove the tenderloins and allow them to rest for 5 minutes before slicing.

Bone-in Loin Roast

Cook Time: 1½ -2 hours
Servings: 8

Ingredients:

- 15 -pound bone-in pork loin roast
- 1/2 cup olive oil
- 1/3 cup fresh rosemary
- 1/3 cup fresh thyme
- 2 tsp salt
- 1 tsp black pepper
- 6 cloves garlic, minced
- 4 lemons, juiced and zested

Method:

1. Remove the pork loin from the fridge, rinse, and pat dry.
2. In a food processor, combine olive oil, herbs, lemon juice and zest, and garlic and pulse to combine into a paste.
3. Slather the pork loin on all sides with the oil and herb mixture and set aside for 30 minutes.
4. Preheat the EGG to 400°F.
5. Place the roast on the grid and close the dome for 1½ hour. The roast is done when a thermometer inserted into the center of the meat reaches 150°F.
6. Remove the roast and allow it to rest for 20 minutes before carving.

Chinese BBQ Pork

Cook Time: 2 day 1 hours 15 minutes
Servings: 4

Ingredients:

- 1 boneless pork roast
- Amber ale -2 tablespoons
- Soy sauce -1/2 cup
- Ketchup -1/2 cup
- Sriracha sauce -1/4 cup
- Brown sugar -1/3 cup
- Chinese rice wine -1/4 cup
- Garlic powder -1/2 teaspoon
- Onion powder -1/2 teaspoon
- Freshly ground black pepper, to taste
- Hoisin sauce -2 tablespoons

Method:

1. For the marinade: In a pan, over moderate-low heat, combine the amber ale with the soy sauce, ketchup, Sriracha, brown sugar, Chinese rice wine, garlic powder, onion powder, black pepper, and hoisin sauce.
2. Cook while stirring until just combined and warm.
3. Pour the marinade into a ziplock bag and add the pork roast making sure it is evenly coated. Squeeze the air from the ziplock bag, and securely seal.
4. Transfer to the fridge for 48 hours to marinate.
5. Add a small, water-filled container to the grill along with several pieces of mesquite chips.
6. Remove the pork from the marinade, shaking off any excess marinade.
7. Turn the pork over every 20 minutes, while basting with the remaining sauce, until the meat registers 145°F (63°C) using an internal thermometer.

Prime Rib Roast

Cook Time: 4 ½ -5 hours
Servings: 8-10

Ingredients:

- 1 14-pound rib roast
- 1/4 cup English Pub Rub

Method:

1. Remove from fridge and allow the roast to come to room temperature, about 30 minutes.
2. Dry the roast with paper towels and season liberally with English Pub Rub.
3. Preheat the EGG to 425°F.
4. Place the roast directly on the grid and close the dome.
5. Cook for 20 minutes per pound, or until the internal temperature reaches 130°F (for medium).
6. Remove from the EGG to 450°F and allow the roast to rest for 30 minutes before carving.

New York Style Pastrami

Cook Time: 8-10 hours

Servings: 8-10

Ingredients:

- 1 (12-lb) whole beef brisket
- 1/4 cup curing salt
- 3 tablespoons garlic, granulated
- 2 tablespoons pickling spice
- 2 tablespoons ground coriander
- 1 cup water
- 3 tablespoons black pepper, coarsely ground
- 1 tablespoon coriander seeds, toasted and ground
- 1 tsp garlic, granulated

Method:

1. Wash the brisket and pat-dry.
2. Trim the fat evenly across the surface of the brisket, leaving 1/2 inch of fat on the meat.
3. In a bowl, combine all cure ingredients. Coat the brisket entirely with the cure.
4. Place the cured brisket in a 2-gallon resealable bag. Refrigerate it for 4 days, turning the brisket 1-2 times per day.
5. After 4 days, remove the brisket from the bag. Wash it well and pat-dry.
6. In a mixing bowl, mix together all of the rub ingredients.
7. Coat the brisket evenly with the rub.
8. Let it sit for at room temperature for 30 minutes before smoking.
9. Preheat the EGG to 250°F. Add 2 cups of soaked wood chips to the lit natural lump charcoal. (We like cherry or hickory.)
10. Set the brisket directly on the grid, fat side up.
11. Smoke the meat for 4-5 hours, or until the internal temperature registers 165°F.
12. Remove the brisket from the smoker.
13. Wrap the brisket tightly in aluminum foil, adding 1/4 cup of water to the pouch before sealing the foil.
14. Place the pastrami back on the grid and cook until the internal temperature registers 190°F.
15. For best results, let the pastrami rest for 20-30 minutes before slicing.

Perfectly Smoked Texas Style Brisket

Cook Time: 8-10 hours (1 hour per lb.)
Servings: 8-10

Ingredients:

- 1 (8-10 lb) brisket
- 1 cup basic barbecue rub

Method:

1. Set the brisket in an aluminum pan, fat side-up.
2. Sprinkle liberally with Basic Barbecue Rub.
3. Cover the aluminum pan and refrigerate for at least 6 hours or overnight.
4. Let the brisket come to room temperature in the aluminum pan for 30 minutes.
5. Preheat the EGG to 250°F adding 2 cups of soaked wood chips to the heated coals.
6. Set the brisket directly on the grid. Close the dome.
7. Begin checking the internal temperature of the brisket after 8 hours. Remove the brisket from the smoker when the internal temperature reaches 190°F
8. Let the meat rest for 15-20 minutes before carving.

Rouladen

Cook Time: 30-45 minutes
Servings: 6

Ingredients:

- 1 (1½-2lb) flank steak
- 1/2 cup chopped onion
- 1/3 cup chopped dill pickle
- 1/4 cup German mustard
- 1/2 tsp salt
- 1/4 tsp pepper
- 6 strips of bacon, separated

Method:

1. In a medium skillet, brown 3 strips of bacon until crisp. Remove from the pan.
2. Remove all by 2 Tablespoon of the bacon fat and cook the onion over medium heat or until the onion is translucent. Set aside to cool.
3. Pound flank steak into an 8 inch by 10 inch rectangle.
4. Spread the meat with the mustard.
5. Top the meat with the onion, dill pickle, and crumbled cooked bacon.
6. Roll the meat around the filling lengthwise.
7. Wrap the roast with the remaining raw bacon and secure with metal skewers.
8. Heat the EGG to 425°F. Place the roast on the grid and cook for 30-45 minutes or until the internal temperature reaches 130°F.
9. Allow the rouladen to rest for 20 minutes before carving.

Holiday Sirloin Roast

Cook Time: 2-3 hours
Servings: 6-8

Ingredients:

- 1 (5-8 lb) sirloin roast
- 1/4 cup Dijon mustard
- 2 tablespoons fresh rosemary, chopped
- 1/2 tsp salt
- 1/4 tsp pepper
- 3 cloves garlic, minced

Method:

1. Bring the roast to room temperature for 30 minutes before cooking.
2. Sprinkle the roast with salt and pepper.
3. Spread liberally with Dijon and press rosemary and garlic into the mustard.
4. Heat the EGG to 325°F.
5. Place the roast directly on the grid and close the dome for 2½ to 3 hours or until the internal temperature reaches 130°F.
6. Remove from the EGG onto a board and allow it to rest for 20 minutes before carving.

Chapter 3: Lamb

Rack Of Lamb With Spicy Tzatziki

Cook Time: 1 hours 20 minutes
Servings: 4-6

Ingredients:

- 2 racks of lamb, frenched
- Freshly squeezed juice of 2 lemons
- Lemon zest of 2 lemons
- Paprika -2 teaspoons
- Fresh mint, chopped -1 tablespoon
- Olive oil -3 tablespoons
- Salt -1 teaspoon
- Black pepper -1 teaspoon
- Harissa -1 cup
- Greek yogurt -1 cup

Method:

1. First, in a bowl, combine the lemon juice with the zest, paprika, mint, olive oil, salt, and black pepper. Put to one side until needed.
2. Approximately 60 minutes before you are ready to grill, place the racks of lamb in a baking dish. Add the marinade to the bowl and massage all over the racks of lamb. Cover with kitchen temperature and marinade for 60 minutes, at room temperature.
3. Place the marinated lamb directly onto the hot grate, bone side facing downwards, and grill over direct heat for 5-7 minutes, until browned.
4. Flip the meat over, meat side facing downwards, and cook for 15-20 minutes, over indirect heat, until the meat registers 130°F (54°C).
5. Remove the lamb from the EGG and allow the meat to rest for several minutes, before cutting into chops.
6. In the meantime, make the dip. In a small bowl, swirl the harissa with the yogurt to combine.
7. Serve the chops with the dip.

Grilled Lamb Chops

Cook Time: 30 minutes
Servings: 2

Ingredients:

- 6 lamb chops, 3/4-ins (1.8-cms) thick, frenched
- Freshly squeezed juice of 1 lemon
- 3 cloves garlic, peeled, chopped
- Rosemary leaves
- Thyme leaves
- Sea salt
- Freshly ground black pepper
- Olive oil

Method:

1. First, add the lemon juice to a large bowl.
2. Add the garlic to the bowl.
3. Grind the rosemary and thyme leaves in a mortar and pestle.
4. Add the ground herbs to the lemon and garlic in the large bowl along with a pinch of salt and a dash of black pepper.
5. Drizzle the oil over the chops, add them to the large bowl and toss to evenly combine.
6. Transfer the chops to a ziplock bag and place in the fridge to marinate, overnight.
7. Grill the lamb chops for 5-6 minutes on each side and serve.

Leg Of Lamb Ina Rosemary And Lemon Marinade

Cook Time: 1 hours 25 minutes
Servings: 10

Ingredients:

- 1 boneless leg of lamb
- 1 large bunch rosemary
- Olive oil -1/8 cup
- Freshly squeezed juice of 2 lemons
- Zest of 2 fresh lemons
- Salt -2 teaspoons
- Black pepper -1 tablespoon

Method:

1. For the marinade: In a food processor, combine the rosemary and oil with the lemon juice, lemon zest, salt, and pepper. Mix until incorporated.
2. Next, cover the lamb with the marinade and place in the fridge for half an hour to marinade.
3. Grill the leg of lamb on indirect heat for 45 minutes, until it achieves an internal temperature of 135°F (57°C).
4. Move the lamb to the direct heat and allow it to continue cooking for an additional 5 minutes on each side.
5. With a foil-lined brick, flatten the meat on the grill, as this will allow the outside of the meat to crisp.
6. Once the meat registers 145°F (63°C) pull the leg off the grill and allow to rest while covered in foil for 8 -1o minutes, this will allow the meat juices to redistribute.
7. Slice the meat against the grain and serve.

Greek Lamb Burgers With Spicy Tzatziki

Cook Time: 35 minutes

Servings: 4-6

Ingredients:

- Ground lamb (1-lb, 0.45-kgs)
- Ground beef (2-lbs, 0.9-kgs)
- 1 cucumber
- 2 handfuls fresh mint
- Greek yogurt -1 cup
- Tabasco sauce -1½ tablespoons
- 2 cloves of garlic, peeled and crushed
- Ground cumin -1/4 teaspoon
- Salt and black pepper
- Feta cheese, crumbled -1/2 cup
- Barbecue rub -1 tablespoon
- 4 brioche buns, split

Method:

1. First, for the tzatziki: Grate the cucumber and drain away any of the excess liquid. Add the grated cucumber to a colander and season with salt.
2. Place a heavy plate on top of the grated cucumber to weigh it down and put to one side for half an hour.
3. In a mixing bowl, add the mint along with the yogurt and Tabasco sauce, garlic and cumin. Taste and season with salt and pepper.
4. Add the cucumber to the mixture and transfer to the fridge to chill, until needed.
5. For the burgers: In a bowl, combine the lamb with the beef, feta, and barbecue rub. Using clean hands from the mixture into 4 patties.
6. When the EGG is at temperature, place the patties directly on the grill and cook for a couple of minutes on each side.
7. Shut the EGG vents and allow the burgers to sit for 5 minutes.
8. Remove the burgers from the EGG and allow to rest for an additional few minutes.
9. Serve the burgers inside the buns with a side of homemade spicy tzatziki.

Herb-Crusted Grilled Leg Of Lamb

Cook Time: 50 minutes

Servings: 10

Ingredients:

- Boneless leg of lamb, trimmed, butterflied (2.5-lbs, 1-kgs)
- Lamb rub -1 tablespoon
- 4 cloves of garlic, peeled, minced
- Freshly squeezed lemon juice -2 tablespoons
- Cilantro -1/2 cup
- Parsley -1/2 cup
- Unsalted butter, softened -6 tablespoons

Method:

1. In a bowl, combine the rub with the garlic, lemon juice, cilantro, parsley, and butter.
2. Coat the lamb in the herb-infused butter
3. Put the leg of lamb directly on the grill and sear on each side for 5 minutes.
4. Close the grill lid and cook for between 3-40 minutes, until the lamb registers an internal temperature of 130°F (54°C).
5. Remove the lamb from the grill and allow to rest for several minutes before cutting and serving.

Chapter 4: Poultry

Southern-Style Grilled Chicken Wings

Cook Time: 45 minutes

Servings: 6-8

Ingredients:

- Whole chicken wings (6-lbs, 2.7-kgs)
- Sea salt -1 tablespoon
- Freshly ground black pepper -1 teaspoon
- Garlic powder -2 teaspoons
- Parsley, chopped, to garnish
- Hot sauce -2/3 cup
- Unsalted butter -3/4 cup
- Runny honey -2 tablespoons
- Apple cider vinegar -2 tablespoons

Method:

1. For the seasoning: In a bowl, combine the salt, with the freshly ground black pepper, and garlic powder. Add the chicken wings to the seasoning and toss to coat evenly.
2. Arrange the wings on the preheated grill in such a way that they are touching one another.
3. Grill the wings for around 20 minutes, turning over every 5 minutes until the meat juices run clear.
4. Meanwhile, prepare the sauce. Over low heat, in a pan, combine the hot sauce, and butter with the honey, and apple cider vinegar, until melted and heated through.
5. Transfer the cooked chicken wings to a bowl.
6. Pour the sauce over the chicken wings, and toss to evenly coat.
7. Return the chicken wings to the grill and cook for a couple of minutes on each side.
8. Toss the wings in the prepared sauce once more, garnish with parsley and enjoy.

Chicken all'Arrabbiata

Cook Time: 1 hours
Servings: 4

Ingredients:

- 6 leg quarters, cut into drumsticks and thighs
- 6 cloves garlic, diced
- 1 small poblano pepper, finely diced
- 1 large yellow pepper, diced
- 1 large onion, diced
- 1 cup dry white wine
- 3 tablespoons olive oil
- 2 tablespoons red wine vinegar
- 1 tablespoon tomato paste
- 1½ tsp crushed red chile flake
- 1 28-ounce can crushed tomatoes
- 1 bay leaf

Method:

1. Preheat The EGG to 500°F with the Dutch oven on the grid.
2. Season chicken on all sides with salt and pepper.
3. Place oil and chicken pieces in the Dutch oven. Brown on all sides.
4. Remove chicken and pour off all but 2 Tablespoon of the remaining oil.
5. Add onion, garlic, crushed red chile flake and cook until softened.
6. Add the bell pepper and poblano pepper and cook until softened.
7. Stir in tomato paste and cook for 1-2 minutes or until the tomato paste begins to darken.
8. Add wine and cook for 2 minutes, scraping the bottom of the Dutch oven.
9. Add tomatoes, vinegar, and chicken back into the pot.
10. Cover, reduce the heat to 400°F, and close the dome for 35 minutes.
11. Remove the bay leaf and serve.

Green Curry Chicken

Cook Time: 40 minutes
Servings: 4

Ingredients:

- 2 lbs boneless skinless chicken breast, cut into 1 inch cubes
- 1 tablespoon garlic, minced
- 1 tablespoon ginger, grated
- 2 green onions, chopped
- 2 cups unsweetened coconut milk
- 2 tablespoon canola oil
- 2 tablespoon soy sauce
- 2 tablespoons cornstarch
- 2 tablespoons Thai green curry paste
- 2 tablespoons brown sugar
- 1 tablespoon fish sauce

Method:

1. Preheat the EGG to 500°F with the Dutch oven on the grid.
2. Dredge chicken breast pieces in soy sauce, then corn starch.
3. Place oil and chicken in the heated Dutch oven and brown. Work in batches, being careful not to overcrowd the pan.
4. Add garlic, ginger, and green onion and stir until fragrant.
5. Add Thai green curry paste, fish sauce, coconut milk, and sugar and stir to combine.
6. Lower the temperature in the EGG to 350°F.
7. Cover the Dutch oven and the dome and simmer for 25-30 minutes.
8. Serve over jasmine rice with lime wedges and whole cilantro leaves.

Rotisserie Chicken

Cook Time: 1-1½ hours

Servings: 6

Ingredients:

- 1 (4-5 lb) whole chicken, gizzards and giblets removed
- 2 quarts warm water
- 1/4 cup kosher salt
- 1/4 cup brown sugar
- 2 Tablespoons whole peppercorns
- 1 lemon, halved
- 2 lbs small waxy potatoes, cut in half (we like Yukon golds)
- 1 lbs carrots, cut into 2 inch chunks
- 1/4 cup butter, softened
- 1 onion, cut into wedges
- 2 sprigs fresh thyme
- 4 whole cloves garlic

Method:

1. Combine brine ingredients until the salt and sugar dissolve and add enough ice to bring the brine to room temperature.
2. Submerge the chicken into the brine and allow to chill in the refrigerator for a minimum of 2 hours and up to overnight.
3. Remove the chicken from the brine and pat dry.
4. In the bottom of a cold Dutch oven, place the vegetables and top with the chicken, breast side up.
5. Gently lift the skin away from the meat and rub butter beneath the skin.
6. Preheat the EGG to 425°F.
7. Cover the Dutch oven and place on the EGG. Lower the dome for 1-1½ hours or until the internal temperature of the meatiest part of the thigh registers 160°F
8. Remove the Dutch oven from the EGG and allow it to sit for an additional 10 minutes before removing the lid.
9. Remove the chicken, place the vegetables on a platter or in a bowl. Carve the chicken and serve.

Chicken Cacciatore

Cook Time: 40 minutes

Servings: 4-6

Ingredients:

- 4 lbs chicken thighs, bone in and skin on
- 1/4 cup freshly chopped basil
- 3 cloves garlic, minced
- 1 bell pepper, sliced
- 1 onion, sliced
- 3/4 cups dry white wine
- 3/4 cups chicken stock
- 1/2 cup flour
- 3 tablespoons olive oil
- 3 tablespoons capers
- 1½ tsp dried oregano
- 1 (28 ounce) can diced tomatoes with juice
- Salt and Pepper

Method:

1. Preheat the EGG to 500°F with the Dutch oven on the grid.
2. Season each chicken piece with salt and pepper and lightly dredge in flour.
3. Place olive oil in the Dutch oven and brown chicken pieces on all sides. Work in batches and set chicken aside.
4. Drain all but 2 Tablespoon of the fat in the Dutch oven and add onion, garlic, and bell pepper and cook until soft.
5. Add chicken back into the pot and add wine and chicken stock, scraping the bottom of the Dutch oven.
6. Add tomatoes, oregano and capers, stir and cover
7. Reduce the heat in the EGG to 400°F and lower the dome for 35 minutes.
8. Garnish with fresh basil and serve.

Braised Chicken Thighs with Mushrooms

Cook Time: 1 hours

Servings: 4

Ingredients:

- 2 lbs chicken thighs, bone in and skin on
- 1 lb mushrooms, thinly sliced
- 1 cup finely chopped onion
- 1 tablespoon butter
- 1 tablespoon fresh thyme, chopped
- 1/2 cup white wine
- 1/2 cup chicken broth
- 1/4 cup flour
- 2 tablespoons olive oil
- Salt and Pepper

Method:

1. Lightly dredge each chicken thigh in flour and season with salt and pepper.
2. Preheat the EGG to 500°F.
3. Place the Dutch oven directly on the grid and allow the pot to heat for 5-7 minutes.
4. Pour olive oil into the oven and add chicken thighs, being careful not to crowd the pan.
5. Brown the chicken thighs in batches until they are golden brown on all sides. Remove from the Dutch oven and set aside.
6. To the pan, add butter and mushrooms, but do not stir for 2-3 minutes or until the mushrooms begin to brown.
7. Add onions and cook until softened.
8. Return the chicken to the pot and add wine, chicken, broth, and thyme.
9. Cover the Dutch oven, reduce the heat of The EGG to 350°F and close the dome.
10. Allow the chicken to cook 30-40 minutes or until the internal temperature reaches 170°F. Serve warm.

Green Chile Chicken Chili

Cook Time: 45 minutes –1 hours
Servings: 8

Ingredients:

- 2 lbs ground chicken
- 1 cup chopped onion
- 1 tablespoon garlic, minced
- 1 quart chicken stock
- 2 tablespoons olive oil
- 1 tablespoon ground cumin
- 1 tablespoon dried oregano
- 4 cans (14.5 ounce) Great Northern Beans, drained and rinsed
- 2 cans (4 ounce) chopped green chiles
- Salt & Pepper

Method:

1. Preheat The EGG to 500°F with the Dutch oven on the grid.
2. Add oil, onion, and garlic to the pot and cook until soft.
3. Add ground chicken, salt and pepper to taste, and cook until brown.
4. Add cumin and oregano and cook for 1 minute.
5. Add chicken stock and green chiles.
6. Reduce the heat in the EGG to 350°F
7. Cover the Dutch oven and lower the dome for 40-50 minutes. Serve hot with shredded cheese and lime wedges.

Glazed And Grilled Sweet Asian Chicken

Cook Time: 35 minutes
Servings: 4

Ingredients:

- 3 large chicken breasts, cut into bite-sized pieces
- Soy sauce -1 tablespoon
- Brown sugar -1/4 cup
- 1 bouillon cube
- Fresh ginger, peeled and finely chopped -1/2 teaspoon
- Water -1/4 cup
- Broccoli, cut into bite-sized pieces -2 cups
- 1 red bell pepper, cut into 1 -ins (2.5-cms)
- 1 medium-size red onion, peeled, cut into 1 -ins (2.5-cms)
- 1 yellow bell pepper, cut into i-ins (2.5-cms)
- Rice or noodles, cooked, to serve

Method:

1. In a mixing bowl, combine the soy sauce with the brown sugar, bouillon cube, ginger, and water.
2. In a heat-safe grill pan combine the chicken with the broccoli, red bell pepper, red onion, and yellow bell pepper.
3. Put the pan on the EGG .
4. Cook for 12-15 minutes, until the chicken juices run clear and the vegg ies are bite tender.
5. Serve with noodles or rice, and enjoy.

Chicken Tacos

Cook Time: 35 minutes
Servings: 8

Ingredients:

- Boneless, skinless chicken thighs (3-lbs, 1.36-kgs)
- Salt and freshly ground black pepper, to season
- Cumin seeds, toasted -2 teaspoons
- 1 red onion, peeled and diced
- 2 cans chopped fire-roasted tomatoes (14.5-ozs, 0.4-kgs each)
- 8 tortillas, warmed
- Sour cream, to serve

Method:

1. Season the chicken thighs with salt and freshly ground black pepper.
2. Arrange the chicken thighs, with their smooth side facing down on the hot grill until light grill marks begin to appear. Turn the chicken over and cook for an additional 5 minutes, until light grill marks appear.
3. Continue grilling, while flipping over every 2-3 minutes, for approximately 10-15 minutes, until the chicken registers an internal temperature of 165°F (74°C) when using a meat thermometer.
4. In a pan on medium-high heat, toast the cumin seeds.
5. Add the onions to the pan and sauté, until just translucent.
6. Add the canned tomatoes to the pan followed by the grilled chicken thighs, and cook until the liquid reduces.
7. Serve the grilled chicken thighs and tomatoes and onions alongside warm tortillas.
8. Serve with sour cream.

Turkey Bacon Dogs

Cook Time: 20 minutes
Servings: 8

Ingredients:

- 1 package bun-size turkey franks (1-lb, 0.45-kgs)
- 8 slices turkey bacon.
- 8 hot dog rolls
- 2/3 cup Monterey Jack cheese, shredded
- Salsa, store-bought
- Jalapeno pepper slices, to serve
- Sour cream, to serve

Method:

1. Wrap each turkey frank with one slice of turkey bacon.
2. Grill the franks, while frequently turning until the bacon is crispy.
3. Put the franks inside the rolls and sprinkle with shredded cheese.
4. Serve with salsa, jalapeno pepper and a dollop of sour cream.

Mexican-Style Turkey Burgers

Cook Time: 30 minutes
Servings: 4

Ingredients:

- 1 turkey breast (1-lb, 0.45-kgs)
- Salsa, store-bought -1/3 cup
- Green onions, chopped -1/4 cup
- Dried oregano leaves -1 teaspoon
- Ground cumin -1/2 teaspoon
- Salt -1/4 teaspoon
- 4 lettuce leaves, washed, dried
- 4 burger buns, split
- 4 slices tomato
- 1 ripe avocado, peeled, pitted, and mashed
- Reduced-fat sour cream -1 tablespoon
- Fresh cilantro, chopped -1 tablespoon
- Freshly squeezed lime juice -1 tablespoon

Method:

1. In a bowl combine the turkey with the salsa, green onions, oregano, cumin and salt and using clean hands shape into 4 equal size patties.
2. Arrange the patties on the preheated grid and grill until cooked through, this will take between 4-5 sides on each side. You will need to flip them over once.
3. In the meantime, in a second bowl combine the avocado with the sour cream, cilantro, and fresh lime juice. Season and put to one side.
4. To assemble, place a leaf of lettuce on the bottom of each burger bun. Top with a slice of tomato, and a serving of avocado mixture.

Turkey Shepherd's Pie

Cook Time: 55 minutes

Servings: 4-6

Ingredients:

- Turkey, cooked -2 cups
- Butter -2 tablespoons
- Yellow onion, chopped -1/2 cup
- Celery, chopped -1/3 cup
- Carrots, chopped -1/3 cup
- 1 garlic clove, peeled and minced
- Green beans -1/2 cup
- Salt -1/2 teaspoon
- Freshly ground black pepper -1/2 teaspoon
- Dried thyme -1/2 tsp
- Dried basil -1/2 teaspoon
- Gravy -1 cup
- Mashed potatoes, prepared -2 cups
- Cheddar cheese, shredded and divided (4-ozs, 113-gms)
- Mozzarella cheese, shredded -1 cup

Method:

1. Melt the butter in a cast iron frying pan or skillet.
2. Add the onion along with the celery and carrots and cook while occasionally stirring until the onion is translucent.
3. Add the garlic and cook for 60 seconds.
4. Next, add the turkey followed by the green beans, salt, pepper, thyme, basil and gravy, and cook until sufficiently heated through.
5. Heat the mash until warm.
6. Add half of the shredded Cheddar and stir to incorporate.
7. Spread the cheesy mash evenly over the turkey filling in the skillet.
8. Scatter the remaining shredded cheese over the top and return the skillet to the EGG, and bake for half an hour.
9. Serve warm.

Chapter 5: Fish

Grouper With Tomato-Basil Sauce

Cook Time: 1 hours 45 minutes
Servings: 2

Ingredients:

- 2 Grouper fish fillets
- Freshly squeezed lemon juice -1 tablespoon
- Fresh rosemary, minced -1½ teaspoons
- Olive oil -1½ teaspoons
- Salt -1/4 teaspoon
- Dash of black pepper
- Tomato, seeded and diced -1/4 cup
- Dried basil -1 teaspoon
- Green onion, chopped -1 tablespoon
- Red wine vinegar -1½ teaspoons
- Orange peel, grated -1/4 teaspoon

Method:

1. First, in a ziplock bag, combine the lemon juice with the rosemary, oil, salt, and pepper.
2. Add the grouper to the bag, seal and turn to evenly coat.
3. Transfer the bag to the fridge for 6 o minutes.
4. Remove the fish from the bag, shake off and discard any excess marinade.
5. Arrange the grouper on the grill grid and grill until it flakes easily when using a fork.
6. In a pan, combine the sauce ingredients (tomato, basil, green onion, red wine vinegar, and grated orange peel). Cook over moderate heat.
7. Pour the sauce over the grouper and enjoy.

Southern Catfish With Homemade Salsa

Cook Time: 1 hours 5 minutes
Servings: 4

Ingredients:

- 4 catfish fillets
- 3 medium tomatoes, chopped
- Onion, peeled, chopped -1/4 cup
- 2 jalapeno peppers, seed and finely chopped
- White wine vinegar -2 tablespoons
- Salt, divided -3 teaspoons
- Chili powder -3 teaspoons
- Paprika -3 teaspoons
- Ground cumin 1½ teaspoons
- Ground coriander -1½ teaspoons
- Cayenne pepper -1 teaspoon
- Garlic powder -1/2 teaspoon

Method:

1. In a bowl, combine the tomatoes with the onion, jalapenos, white wine vinegar, and 1 teaspoon of salt. Cover the bowl and transfer to the fridge for a minimum of half an hour.
2. In a second bowl, combine the chili powder, paprika, cumin, coriander, cayenne pepper, garlic powder, and remaining salt. Rub the mixture all over the fish.
3. Grill the fish on the grid, until it flakes easily when using a fork.
4. Serve the fish with the salsa and enjoy.

Grilled Tuna With Chili Orange Marinade

Cook Time: 40 minutes
Servings: 4

Ingredients:

- 4 medium tuna steaks
- Zest and freshly squeezed juice of 1 orange
- 2 cloves garlic, peeled and crushed
- Ground cumin -1/2 teaspoon
- 1 red chili, seeded and grated
- Pinch of sea salt
- Cilantro, freshly chopped, to serve -1 tablespoon
- 1 orange, cut into wedges
- Sugar snap peas, to serve, optional
- Rice, to serve, optional

Method:

1. To prepare the marinade: In a bowl combine the orange zest with the freshly squeezed orange juice, garlic and ground cumin followed by the chili and a pinch of sea salt. Mix thoroughly to combine.
2. Carefully pat the marinade onto the tuna steaks and put aside side to marinate for 30 minutes.
3. Arrange the tuna steaks on the grill and grill for 1-2 minutes on each side. Season with salt during grilling.
4. Garnish with cilantro and oranges and serve with sugar snap peas and rice.

Spicy scallops In Coconut milk

Cook Time: 35 minutes
Servings: 4

Ingredients:

- 12-16 large sea scallops, prepared
- Fennel seeds -1 teaspoon
- Yellow or black mustard seeds -1/2 teaspoon
- Cardamom seeds -1/4 teaspoon
- 4 cloves garlic, peeled, finely chopped
- 2 dried red cayenne chilies with seeds, stemmed, roughly chopped
- Sea salt -1 teaspoon
- Canola oil -2 tablespoons
- Unsweetened coconut milk -1/2 cup
- Cilantro leaves with stems, chopped - 1 tablespoon

Method:

1. For the spice blend: Add the fennel, and mustard, along with the cardamom seeds to a coffee or spice grinder, and grind to a fine pepper-like consistency. Transfer the spice blend to a bowl.
2. To the spice blend, add the scallops, garlic, chilies and sea salt and stir to combine. The scallops must be evenly and thoroughly coated in the mixture.
3. Cover the bowl and transfer the scallops to the fridge until needed.
4. To cook the scallops: Heat the oil in a pan until it shimmers.
5. In a single layer, add the scallops along with the rub to the pan.
6. Sear the scallops for 2-3 minutes on each side, or until a light reddish shade of brown.
7. Stir in the coconut milk, while at the same time scraping any browned bits from the bottom of the pan to deglaze, and cook for 2 minutes, until the scallops are firm.
8. Serve and enjoy.

Pinot Grigio wine large oysters

Cook Time: 35 minutes
Servings: 4

Ingredients:

- 12 large oysters, shucked
- Red onions, peeled, chopped -1/2 cup
- Butter -1/4 cup
- Pinot Grigio wine -1/2 cup
- 4 garlic cloves, peeled
- Spinach, roughly chopped -2½ cups
- Heavy cream -2 tablespoons
- Clam juice -2 tablespoons
- Mozzarella cheese -1/2 cup
- Bacon, crisp, finely chopped -2 tablespoons

Method:

1. In a grill safe pan, set over moderately high heat, saute the onions in 2 tablespoons of butter, until just translucent.
2. Pour in the wine and simmer for a couple of minutes.
3. Add the remaining butter along with the garlic and cook for 60 seconds.
4. Add the spinach, and cook until wilted.
5. Next, add the heavy cream followed by the clam juice, and cook for 3-4 seconds.
6. To serve: Top the oysters with the spinach mixture. Add the mozzarella cheese and place directly on the cooking grid until the cheese begins to bubble, for 4-5 minutes.
7. Scatter the bacon over the top and serve.

Foil Packet Fish Filets

Cook Time: 12-15 minutes
Servings: 4

Ingredients:

- 4 (4 oz each) white fish filets
- 1/2 cup white wine
- 4 tablespoons butter
- 4 pieces heavy duty foil
- 4 sprigs fresh thyme
- 4 green onions, cut in thirds
- 1 zucchini, julienned
- 1 large carrot, julienned
- 1 clove garlic, minced

Method:

1. On the bottom of each foil sheet, place zucchini, carrot and onion to create a bed.
2. Place one fish filet on each bed of vegetables and top with garlic, thyme, 1 Tbs of butter, salt and pepper to taste.
3. Gather two sides of the foil together and fold down so the foil is almost touching the food.
4. Roll one side of the foil then pour in 2 Tablespoon of white wine. Close the remaining side. Repeat
5. Preheat the EGG to 375°F with the convEGGtor® in place.
6. Place the foil packets on the grid and close the dome for 12-15 minutes or until the fish is cooked through.

Cedar Plank Salmon

Cook Time: 25-30 minutes
Servings: 4

Ingredients:

- 4(4-6 oz each) salmon filets
- 2 cedar planks, soaked in water for 3 o minutes
- 1/2 tsp salt
- 1/4 tsp black pepper
- 1/2 cup raspberry preserves
- 2 Tablespoons balsamic vinegar
- 1 jalapeno, chopped
- 1 clove garlic, minced

Method:

1. Season salmon on both sides with salt and pepper.
2. Preheat the EGG to 350°F.
3. Place the plans on the grid and close the dome for 3 minutes.
4. Flip the planks and place the salmon on the heated side. Close the dome for 20 minutes.
5. Meanwhile, combine preserves, vinegar, jalapeño, and garlic in a small sauce pan and heat over low for 10 minutes, stirring occasionally.
6. Brush the salmon with the sauce and close the dome for another 5 minutes.
7. Serve with additional sauce.

Greek Sea Bass

Cook Time: 12-15 minutes
Servings: 4

Ingredients:

- 2 whole sea bass (approximately 1 pound each), cleaned and gutted
- 1/4 cup olive oil
- 2 tablespoons lemon juice
- 2 tablespoons capers
- 2 tablespoons parsley, chopped
- 1 tsp fresh oregano, chopped
- 1/2 tsp salt
- 1/4 tsp dried chili flakes
- 4 cloves garlic
- 1 lemon, thinly sliced

Method:

1. Whisk together herbs, lemon juice, capers, olive oil, salt, and chili flakes. Set aside.
2. Season the sea bass with salt and pepper on the inside cavity and place lemon slices inside.
3. Preheat the EGG to 400°F
4. Place whole fish on the grid and close the dome for 6 minutes.
5. Gently flip the fish and replace the dome for an additional 6-8 minutes or until the fish is cooked through.
6. Remove the sea bass and drizzle with herb and lemon mixture. Serve more on the side for dressing as the fish is eaten.

Grilled Whole Trout

Cook Time: 15-20 minutes
Servings: 2

Ingredients:

- 2 whole trout (about 1 lb each), cleaned and gutted
- 2 tablespoons olive oil
- 1/2 tsp salt
- 1/4 tsp pepper
- 4 cloves garlic, smashed
- 1/2 sliced lemon
- 1/2 bunch fresh parsley

Method:

1. Brush the inside of the cavity and outside of the fish with olive oil and season with salt and pepper.
2. Stuff lemon, garlic, and parsley inside the cavity of each fish.
3. Preheat the EGG to 400°F.
4. Place the fish directly on the grid and close the dome for 10 minutes.
5. Gently flip the fish and close the dome for an additional 5-10 minutes or until the fish is cooked through.

Lemon Bed Cod

Cook Time: 15 minutes
Servings: 6

Ingredients:

- 6 cod filets
- 3 lemons, sliced 1/4 inch thick
- 1 onion, thinly sliced
- Salt & Pepper to taste

Method:

1. Place lemon slices directly on the grid so they are shingled one on top of another.
2. Place onion slices on top of the lemon.
3. Preheat the EGG to 400°F.
4. Season both sides of the cod filets with salt and pepper and place them on top of the onion and lemon beds.
5. Close the dome for 12-15 minutes to allow the lemons to steam the fish.
6. Remove the fish on their lemon beds when the fish is opaque. Serve.

Grilled Tilapia "Ceviche"

Cook Time: 5-6 minutes
Servings: 4

Ingredients:

- 1 lb tilapia filets
- 1/4 cup chopped fresh parsley
- 1/4 cup chopped fresh cilantro
- 1/4 cup freshly squeezed lime juice
- 2 tablespoons olive oil
- 1/2 tsp red chile flakes
- 5 green onions, minced
- 2 tomatoes, diced
- 2 stalks celery, sliced
- 1/2 green bell pepper, minced
- Salt & pepper to taste

Method:

1. Mix lime juice, olive oil, vegetables and herbs together in a large bowl.
2. Preheat the EGG to 400°F.
3. Season both sides of the tilapia with salt and pepper and place on the grid.
4. Close the dome and cook for 3 minutes.
5. Gently flip the fish and cook for another 2-3 minutes or until the fish is opaque. Set aside.
6. Flake apart the tilapia filets and gently stir into the vegetable mixture to combine.
7. Serve room temperature or chilled.

Grilled shrimp

Cook Time: 30 minutes
Servings: 4-6

Ingredients:

- Jumbo shrimp, peeled, deveined (1.5-lbs, 3.8-kgs)
- Nonstick cooking spray
- Fresh flat-leaf parsley, finely chopped -1/4 cup
- Red onion, peeled, finely chopped -1/4 cup
- Lemon rind, grated -1 tablespoon
- Fresh oregano, finely chopped -1 tablespoon
- Garlic, peeled, minced -1 teaspoon
- Extra-virgin olive oil, divided -2½ tablespoons
- Runny honey -1 tablespoon
- Freshly ground black pepper -1/2 teaspoon
- Kosher salt -1/4 teaspoon

Method:

1. In a bowl, combine the first 5 ingredients (parsley, red onion, lemon rind, oregano, and garlic).
2. In a second, larger bowl combine the shrimp with 1 tablespoon of oil, honey, pepper, and salt and gently toss to coat evenly.
3. Arrange the shrimp on the grill rack and grill for a few minutes on each side, until sufficiently cooked through. Remove the shrimp.
4. Stir the remaining oil along with the vinegar into the herb mixture.
5. Toss the shrimp in the mixture to evenly coat.
6. Serve and enjoy.

Chapter 6: Vegetables

Mexican Cobb Salad

Cook Time: 1 hours 55 minutes
Servings: 2-4

Ingredients:

- 2 ears fresh corn, silk, and husks removed
- 2 large jalapeno peppers
- 1 red bell pepper, stemmed, seeded, and quartered
- 1 medium red onion, peeled, sliced 1/2-ins (1.27-cms) thick
- Freshly squeezed lime juice, to taste
- Sea salt, to season
- 4 cups romaine lettuce, sliced -4 cups
- Walnuts, toasted, coarsely chopped - 1 cup
- Pepper Jack cheese, cut into small cubes -1 cup
- Canned black beans, rinsed, drained -1 cup
- Salad dressing, of choice

Method:

1. Arrange the corn, peppers, and onion on your EGG and grill until lightly charred all over. Remove the veggies from the EGG.
2. Cut the kernels off the cob, thinly slice the jalapeno pepper and cut the bell pepper and onion into bite-sized strips. Drizzle with fresh lime juice and season with salt. Set aside to cool.
3. Evenly pile the lettuce into 4 individual salad bowls.
4. In rows, top with equal amounts of grilled veggies, toasted walnuts, Pepper Jack cheese, and black beans.
5. Serve with your favorite dressing and enjoy.

Asian-Style Asparagus

Cook Time: 25 minutes
Servings: 4

Ingredients:

- 16 thick asparagus spears
- Low sodium soy sauce -1 tablespoon
- Dark sesame oil -1 teaspoon
- 1 clove garlic, peeled, minced
- Sesame seeds, toasted -2 teaspoons
- Black pepper - 1/4 teaspoon
- Pinch of sea salt

Method:

1. First, snap the tough ends off the asparagus.
2. Place the asparagus on a clean, flat surface.
3. Thread cocktail sticks horizontally through the spears 1-ins (2.5-cms) from each end to create a raft shape. Repeat until all the asparagus are prepared.
4. In a bowl, combine the soy sauce with the sesame oil, and garlic.
5. Brush the soy sauce mixture over the asparagus rafts to evenly coat.
6. Grill the asparagus for 3 minutes on both sides, until crisp-tender.
7. Scatter with toasted sesame seeds and season with black pepper and a pinch of sea salt.

Garlic Green Beans

Cook Time: 55 minutes
Servings: 8

Ingredients:

- Fresh green beans, trimmed (2-lbs, 0.9-kgs)
- Olive oil -1/2 cup
- Garlic, peeled, minced -2 teaspoons
- Kosher salt -2 teaspoons

Method:

1. In a mixing bowl, combine the green beans with the olive oil, garlic and kosher salt, and toss well to evenly and entirely coat. Set the green beans aside for 3 0 minutes, to marinate.
2. In a single layer, arrange the green beans, in a heat-safe grill pan.
3. Place the pan on the hot grill and cook, while stirring for 8-10 minutes, until the green beans are lightly charred.
4. Remove from the pan and serve.

Chapter 7: Appetizers

Bacon Mac And Cheese

Cook Time: 25 minutes
Servings: 4

Ingredients:

- 12 rashers uncooked bacon
- Olive oil -1 tablespoon
- Panko breadcrumbs -1 cup
- Uncooked macaroni -3 cups
- Plain Greek yogurt -1/2 cup
- Mayonnaise -1/4 cup
- Mature cheddar cheese, freshly grated -2 cups
- Cider vinegar -2 tablespoons
- Hot sauce -2 teaspoons
- Dijon mustard -1 teaspoon
- 1 garlic clove, peeled, coarsely chopped Salt -1/2 teaspoon
- Freshly ground black pepper -1/2 teaspoon
- Cheddar cheese, grated

Method:

1. Heat the oil on the preheated grill in a heat-safe grill pan.
2. Add the breadcrumbs to the pan and stir until golden, for 90 seconds. Scrape the breadcrumbs into a bowl and set to one side.
3. Add the bacon to the pan, and cook until crispy. Transfer to a kitchen paper towel lined plate to drain, and crumble.
4. In a large pan of salted boiling water cook the pasta until al dente. Drain and rinse under cold running water, to cool.
5. While the macaroni cooks in a food blender, combine the Greek yogurt with the mayonnaise. Add the grated Cheddar followed by the vinegar, hot sauce, Dijon mustard, garlic, salt, and black pepper. Process the ingredients until a smooth mayonnaise-like consistency. Stir and scrape down the sides of the blender jug as necessary.
6. In a large mixing bowl, toss the drained pasta with the yogurt mixture to evenly coat.
7. Serve with a sprinkle of Cheddar and toasted breadcrumbs.

Italian-Style Blue Cheese Stuffed Portabella Mushrooms

Cook Time: 40 minutes

Servings: 2

Ingredients:

- 4 large Portabella mushrooms, stemmed
- Italian dressing, store-bought -3 cups
- Blue cheese -2 cups

Method:

1. Marinate the mushrooms in the store-bought Italian dressing for half an hour.
2. Remove the mushrooms from the marinade and place on the grill, gill side facing downwards for a few minutes.
3. Flip the mushrooms over. Place the blue cheese in the mushroom caps and grill for an additional 3 minutes.
4. Serve either whole or cut into wedges with cocktail sticks.

Garlic Toast

Cook Time: 10 minutes
Servings: 2-4

Ingredients:

- 1 large French loaf
- Garlic olive oil -1/2 cup
- Sea salt, to season
- Parsley chopped, to garnish

Method:

1. Slice the loaf into equal portions of approximately 1-ins (2.5-cms) thick.
2. Coat the slices of bread on one side only with garlic olive oil and sea salt.
3. Arrange the slices on the EGG and toast, for 5 minutes.
4. Garnish with chopped parsley.
5. Serve and enjoy.

Chapter 8: Side & Salads

Bacon Wrapped Pineapple

Cook Time: 10 minutes
Servings: 6

Ingredients:

- 1 cup Classic Texas Barbecue Sauce (or your favorite sauce)
- 1 lb bacon, cut into 4 inch strips
- 1 pineapple cut into 2 inch cubes

Method:

1. Wrap each pineapple piece with a 4 inch strip of bacon and secure with a toothpick.
2. Place on the grid of a 425°F EGG and close the dome for 8 minutes or until the bacon is crispy.
3. Brush each pineapple chunk with barbecue sauce and close the dome for another 2 minutes.
4. Serve warm with additional barbecue sauce for dipping.

Baba Ganoush

Cook Time: 6-10 minutes
Servings: 8

Ingredients:

- 2 Tablespoons fresh parsley
- 1 egg plant, sliced into 1/2 inch rounds
- 1 clove garlic
- The juice and zest of 1 lemon
- 2 Tablespoons olive oil
- 2 Tablespoons tahini
- Salt & Pepper

Method:

1. Brush both sides of each egg plant slice with olive oil and season with salt and pepper.
2. Place on a 425°F EGG and close the dome for 3-5 minutes.
3. Flip the egg plant and close the dome for another 3-5 minutes.
4. Peel the egg plant skins away from the flesh and discard.
5. In a food processor, combine egg plant, tahini, parsley, garlic, lemon zest and lemon juice and puree until smooth.
6. Taste for seasoning and add salt and pepper accordingly.
7. Serve at room temperature with pita chips, pretzels, or raw vegetables.

Cowboy Caviar

Cook Time: 10 minutes
Servings: 8

Ingredients:

- 2 ears fresh corn on the cob
- 1 large tomato, finely diced
- 1 bell pepper, finely diced
- 1 jalapeño, very finely chopped
- 1/4 cup bottled Italian salad dressing (or make your own)
- 2 cans black beans, drained and rinsed
- 1 can pinto beans, drained and rinsed

Method:

1. Place shucked and cleaned ears of corn on a 425°F EGG and close the dome for 5 minutes.
2. Turn the corn and close the dome for another 5 minutes before removing and setting aside.
3. Carefully cut the corn off the cob and place it in a large bow.
4. Add remaining ingredients and toss to combine.

Alligator Egg s

Cook Time: 10 minutes
Servings: 6

Ingredients:

- 8 ounces cream cheese, softened
- 1 cup sharp cheddar cheese
- 12 thin slices bacon
- 6 jalapeños

Method:

1. Slice jalapeños in half and remove seeds. Set aside.
2. In a small bowl, combine cheddar cheese and cream cheese until mixed.
3. Stuff 2 Tablespoon of the cream cheese mixture into each jalapeño half.
4. Wrap each jalapeño half in one strip of bacon, securing with a toothpick.
5. Preheat the EGG to 425°F.
6. Place the alligator egg s directly on the grid and close the dome for 10 minutes or until the bacon is crisp. Serve immediately.

Grilled Lemon Garlic Zucchini

Cook Time: 5 minutes

Servings: 6-8

Ingredients:

- 4 zucchini, sliced lengthwise into 1/2 inch slices
- 1/4 cup butter, softened
- 2 tsp parsley, chopped
- 3 cloves garlic, minced
- The zest and juice of 1 lemon

Method:

1. In a small dish, combine butter, parsley, garlic, lemon zest, and lemon juice.
2. Liberally brush each zucchini slice with the butter mixture.
3. Place the zucchini on a 500°F EGG and close the dome for 3 minutes.
4. Flip the zucchini and recover with the dome for an additional 2 minutes.
5. Drizzle remaining butter on top of zucchini as it comes off the grill. Serve warm.

Broiled Tomatoes and Parmesan

Cook Time: 5 minutes

Servings: 4

Ingredients:

- 1/4 cup parmesan, shredded
- 4 roma tomatoes
- 1 tablespoon olive oil
- 1 tsp red wine vinegar
- Salt & Pepper

Method:

1. Cut each tomato in half, lengthwise, and brush with olive oil.
2. Place in a 500°F EGG and lower the dome for 2 minutes.
3. Turn the tomatoes, season with vinegar, salt, and pepper and top with parmesan cheese.
4. Lower the dome for an additional 2 minutes on until the cheese melts. Serve warm.

Grilled Cabbage with Champagne Vinaigrette

Cook Time: 10 minutes
Servings: 6-8

Ingredients:

- 1 head cabbage
- 2 tablespoons olive oil
- Salt and Pepper
- 1/2 cup olive oil
- 1/4 cup Champagne vinegar
- 2 tablespoons capers in brine, drained
- 1 tablespoon Dijon mustard
- 1 shallot, finely chopped

Method:

1. Cut the cabbage into 1/2 inch "steaks" from top to root.
2. Brush each side with olive oil and season with salt and pepper.
3. Place on a 425°F EGG and close the lid for 5 minutes.
4. Meanwhile, in a small bowl, combine shallot, mustard, capers, and vinegar.
5. While whisking, stream in olive oil until dressing emulsifies.
6. Flip cabbage steaks and cook on the other side for an additional 5 minutes with the dome closed.
7. Remove cabbage from the grill to a platter and pour dressing over top. Serve warm.

Chapter 9: Desserts

S'mores Ina Sugar Cone

Cook Time: 20 minutes
Servings: 15

Ingredients:

- 15 large marshmallows
- 15 sugar cones
- 15 squares of milk or dark chocolate

Method:

1. Place one marshmallow along with one square of chocolate in a sugar cone.
2. Arrange the cones on the grilling rack and position the stone on the EGG .
3. Cook for 8-10 minutes, until the marshmallows
4. are brown and gooey, and the chocolate is beginning to melt.
5. Enjoy.

Chocolate Chip Cookie Peanut Butter Cup S'Mores

Cook Time: 5 minutes

Servings: 4

Ingredients:

- 8 chocolate chip cookies
- 4 peanut butter cup candies
- 4 marshmallows

Method:

1. On the grid of a 225°F EGG, place one cookie, flat side up, with one peanut butter cup candy and one marshmallow on top.
2. Close the dome for 5 minutes or until the marshmallow begins to puff.
3. Close the s'more with the other chocolate chip cookie and get ready for the sugar rush.

Apple Pizza

Cook Time: 5 minutes
Servings: 8

Ingredients:

- 1 pizza dough
- 1 cup apple pie filling
- 1/4 cup vanilla cake mix
- 2 Tablespoon melted butter
- Vanilla Ice Cream

Method:

1. Stretch pizza dough into a 14 "round and place on a pizza peel.
2. In a small bowl, combine cake mix and melted butter until it forms a crumbly texture.
3. Spread apple pie filling over pizza dough and top with crumb mixture.
4. Bake on a pizza stone in a 500°F EGG for 5 minutes.
5. Slice and serve with vanilla frosting.

Grilled Pineapple Sundaes

Cook Time: 5 minutes
Servings: 4

Ingredients:

- 4 fresh pineapple spears
- Vanilla Ice Cream
- Jarred Caramel Sauce
- Toasted Coconut

Method:

1. Place pineapple spears on a 400°F EGG and close the dome for 2 minutes.
2. Turn the pineapple and close the dome for another 2 minutes.
3. Turn the pineapple once more and close the dome for another minute.
4. Serve pineapple topped with ice cream, caramel sauce, and toasted coconut.

Grilled Coconut And Rum French Toast

Cook Time: 30 minutes
Servings: 4

Ingredients:

- 1 Challah loaf, sliced into 1/2-ins (1.25-cms) slices
- 4 medium egg s
- 2 tbsp whole milk
- Coconut rum -2 tablespoons
- Dash of ground cinnamon
- Canola oil
- Strawberries, hulled, sliced, to serve
- Whipped cream, to serve

Method:

1. In a bowl, combine the egg s with the milk, rum, and cinnamon.
2. In the meantime, while the EGG is heating, add the slices of bread to the egg-cinnamon mixture and allow to soak.
3. Coat the grill grid with canola oil, arrange the soaked bread on the grill and grill for 4 minutes, on each side, until charred marks begin to form.
4. Serve the toast with strawberries and lashings of whipped cream.

Fresh Peach Crisp

Cook Time: 5 minutes
Servings: 4

Ingredients:

- 2 peaches, halved with pits removed
- Vanilla Ice Cream
- 1 cup good quality granola

Method:

1. Place the peach halves, cut side down, on a 400°F EGG and cover with the dome for 5 minutes.
2. Remove the peaches and place them, cut side up, in a bowl. Top with vanilla ice cream and granola.

Banana Boats

Cook Time: 10 minutes
Servings: 4

Ingredients:

- 4 green bananas
- Chocolate chips
- Miniature marshmallows
- Peanut butter chips
- Crushed cookies

Method:

1. Split a banana lengthwise from end to end leaving the peel intact on the opposite side.
2. Top with desired toppings.
3. Wrap the banana in heavy duty aluminum foil.
4. Place the bananas on a 400°F EGG and close the dome for 10 minutes
5. Unwrap and serve topped with vanilla ice cream, whipped cream, or by themselves

Grilled Plums with Honey and Ricotta

Cook Time: 5 minutes

Servings: 4

Ingredients:

- 4 plums, cut in half and pitted
- 1/2 cup whole milk ricotta cheese
- 2 Tablespoons honey
- 1/4 tsp cracked black pepper

Method:

1. Place the plums, cut side down on a 400°F EGG
2. Close the dome for 5 minutes.
3. Serve the plums, cut side up, with a dollop of ricotta, a drizzle of honey, and a sprinkling of cracked black pepper.

Pineapple Upside-Down Cake

Cook Time: 30 minutes
Servings: 6

Ingredients:

- Light brown sugar, firmly packed - 1/2 cup +1/2 cup
- Canned sweetened condensed milk (14-ozs, 0.4kgs)
- 7 fresh pineapple slices, peeled and cut into 1/4 ins (0.64-cms) thick
- All-purpose flour -1½ cups
- Baking powder -1½ teaspoons
- Table salt -1/4 teaspoon
- Unsalted butter -1 cup
- 3 large-size egg s
- 5 large-size egg yolks
- Vanilla essence -1½ teaspoons
- Granulated sugar -1 cup
- 7 maraschino cherries

Method:

1. In a bowl, combine 1/2 cup of brown sugar with the milk and stir to incorporate.
2. Cut a hole - approximately the same diameter as the maraschino cherries - in the middle of each pineapple slice.
3. Dredge the pineapple in the sugar-milk mixture and arrange them on the grill grid.
4. Close the EGG 'S lid and cook for a couple of minutes on each side.
5. Transfer the grilled pineapple to a plate and allow to cool.
6. In a second bowl, sift the flour with the baking powder and salt. Set to one side.
7. In a pan, melt the butter. Set aside to cool.
8. In a third bowl, whisk the whole egg s with the yolks. Add the vanilla essence along with the remaining brown sugar and granulated sugar. Stir to incorporate entirely.
9. Gradually add the flour mixture to the egg followed by the melted butter and mix thoroughly.
10. Arrange the slices of pineapple in the bottom of a greased 9 " circular cake pan.
11. Arrange a cherry to sit in the middle of each ring.
12. Pour the batter evenly over the pineapple and with a spatula, smooth the batter until evenly spread.

13. Place the pan on the cooking grid.
14. Close the EGG's lid and cook for 30-35 minutes, until springy to the touch.
15. Remove the pan and allow to cool for several minutes.
16. Gently run a blunt knife around the inside rim of the cake pan.
17. Invert the pan onto a serving platter.
18. Serve and enjoy.

Chapter 10: Pizza and Burgers

Italian Ham Pizza

Cook Time: 15 minutes
Servings: 4-8

Ingredients:

- 4 slices of Parma ham
- 1 store-bought, family-size pizza dough base
- Tomato-based pizza sauce, store-bought -1/2 cup
- 1/2 buffalo mozzarella ball, torn
- 5 Kalamata olives, pitted and sliced
- Mature Cheddar cheese -3 tablespoons
- Olive oil
- Flour, to dust
- 8 basil leaves

Method:

1. Shape and place the pizza dough directly onto a pizza peel.
2. With a ladle, put the pizza sauce in the center of the pizza base and evenly spread it around towards the edge, leaving a small gap around the rim.
3. Distribute the ham, mozzarella, olives and grated Cheddar over the base.
4. Brush the unfilled rim of the pizza with a drop of olive oil.
5. Sprinkle a little flour on the pizza stone.
6. Using the pizza peel carefully transfer the pizza to the pizza stone.
7. Close the EGG 'S lid and cook for between 6-8 minutes, until the cheese is melted and the crust golden.
8. Scatter with basil leaves, drizzle with olive oil and enjoy.

Buffalo Chicken Pizza

Ingredients:

- 1 pizza dough
- 1/4 cup Franks Buffalo Sauce
- 1 cup shredded provolone cheese
- 1/2 cup cooked chicken
- 1/4 cup sliced celery
- 1/4 cup crumbled blue cheese

Method:

1. Stretch dough to 14" and place on pizza peel.
2. Spread dough with Frank's Buffalo Sauce.
3. Top with provolone and cooked chicken.
4. Cook according to desired method.
5. When pizza comes out, top with sliced celery and crumbled blue cheese.

Classic Meat Lovers Pizza

Ingredients:

- 1 pizza dough
- 1/4 cup basic pizza sauce
- 1 cup mozzarella cheese
- 1/4 cup cooked Italian sausage
- 1/4 cup chopped ham
- 12 slices pepperoni
- 6 slices salami

Method:

1. Stretch pizza dough to 14" and place on a pizza peel.
2. Top with sauce, cheese, and meats.
3. Cook according to desired method.

Chicken Bacon Artichoke Pizza

Ingredients:

- 1 pizza dough
- 2 Tablespoon olive oil
- 1 clove garlic, minced
- 1/4 tsp black pepper
- 1/2 cup shredded mozzarella cheese
- 1/2 cup shredded provolone cheese
- 1/2 cup cooked chicken
- 1/4 cup marinated artichoke hearts, chopped
- 2 Tablespoons crumbled bacon

Method:

1. Stretch dough to 14 "and place on pizza peel.
2. Spread dough with olive oil, garlic, and black pepper.
3. Top with provolone, mozzarella, chicken, artichoke hearts, and bacon.
4. Cook according to desired method.

Basic Pizza Sauce

Ingredients:

- 2 tablespoons olive oil
- 1 tsp basil
- 1 tsp oregano
- 1 can (28 ounces) crushed tomatoes
- 1 small white onion, finely diced
- 1 clove garlic, minced

Method:

1. In a medium saucepan, heat olive oil over medium.
2. Saute onion and garlic for 10 minutes or until translucent.
3. Add tomatoes, basil, and oregano and simmer for 10 minutes. Set aside to cool.
4. Can be kept in the fridge for up to 1 week or frozen for up to 3 months.

Garlic Clam Pizza

Ingredients:

- 1 pizza dough
- 2 Tablespoon olive oil
- 1/4 tsp dried oregano
- 3 large garlic cloves, minced
- Salt & Pepper
- 2 cups baby arugula
- 1/2 cup mozzarella cheese
- 2 Tablespoons parmesan
- 2 Tablespoons olive oil
- 2 (6.5-ounce) cans chopped clams, juice drained and reserved
- The juice of 1 lemon

Method:

1. Stretch pizza dough to 14" and place on a pizza peel.
2. Spread the dough with olive oil and top with chopped garlic, oregano, salt, and pepper.
3. Top with cheeses and clams.
4. Cook according to desired method.
5. When the pizza comes out, top with arugula, lemon juice, some of the reserved clam juice, and olive oil.

Prosciutto Cheese Dogs

Cook Time: 25 minutes
Servings: 6

Ingredients:

- 4 slices of prosciutto
- 6 hot dogs
- Italian seasoning, store-bought -1 teaspoon
- 3 pieces stringy cheese
- Olive oil -2 teaspoons
- 6 whole-wheat hot dog rolls
- Dijon mustard
- Tomato, chopped

Method:

1. Slice the hot dogs, lengthwise down the center of each one. Take care not to cut through the ends or bottom.
2. Season the hot dogs with the Italian seasoning, rolling to evenly coat.
3. Pull each piece of string cheese vertically in half, to create 6 pieces.
4. Stuff one cheese portion into each of the hot dog slits.
5. Wrap one slice of prosciutto around each stuffed hot dog, to completely encase.
6. Lightly brush the prosciutto with oil.
7. Arrange the hot dogs in a single layer on a baking sheet.
8. Cook for between 10-12 minutes, until the cheese entirely melts and the ingredients are heated through.
9. Place the hot dogs in the rolls and top with a dollop of mustard, and slices of tomato.

Jalapeno And Cherry Cola Glazed Ham Steaks

Cook Time: 40 minutes

Servings: 4

Ingredients:

- 4 ham steaks (1-lbs, 0.45-kgs)
- Cherry cola, any brand -1 cup
- Firmly packed browned sugar -1 cup
- 4 red jalapenos with seeds, chopped
- Cornstarch -4 tablespoons
- Grenadine -4 tablespoons
- Olive oil -2 tablespoons
- Fresh ground black pepper

Method:

1. For the marinade: In a pan on the stovetop combine the cola with the brown sugar and jalapenos and simmer for approximately 10 minutes.
2. Using a metal fork, mix the cornstarch with the grenadine, and stir into the cola mixture, whisking for 60 seconds, until thickened.
3. Pour the hot glaze into a food processor bowl and using the steel blade, process for 30 seconds.
4. Transfer the glaze to a bowl and put to one side.
5. Brush the ham steak with the olive oil and season with freshly ground black pepper.
6. Arrange the steaks on the grid. Close the EGG 'S lid and cook for 5 minutes, flip the steaks over and baste with additional glaze. Continue to cook for an additional 5 minutes.
7. Transfer the ham steaks to a serving platter and baste with the glaze.
8. Pour the remaining glaze into a dish.
9. Serve the steaks with the glaze.

Quesadilla Burger

Cook Time: 10-12 minutes
Servings: 4

Ingredients:

- 2 lbs ground beef
- 2 tablespoons adobo rub
- 1 cup shredded cheddar cheese
- 4 large flour tortillas
- Sour cream
- Guacamole
- Salsa

Method:

1. Form ground beef into four patties and season both sides with Adobo Rub.
2. Serve each burger with sour cream, guacamole, and salsa.
3. Preheat the EGG to 500°F.
4. Place burgers on the grid and close the dome for 3 minutes.
5. Flip burgers and close the dome for 2 more minutes.
6. Close all of the vents and allow the burgers to sit for 5 minutes.
7. Remove burgers and place flour tortillas on the grid.
8. Top each tortilla with shredded cheese and close the dome for 1 minute until the cheese melts.
9. Place a hamburger in the center of each tortilla and begin folding the tortilla around the burger like an envelope.

Breakfast Burger

Cook Time: 11-13 minutes
Servings: 4

Ingredients:

- 1½ ground beef
- 1/2 lb ground pork breakfast sausage
- 2 tablespoon butter
- 8 strips bacon
- 4 slices sharp cheddar cheese
- 4 Brioche buns
- 4 egg s
- 4 thick slices tomato

Method:

1. In a medium bowl, mix ground beef and sausage until just combined.
2. Form into 4 patties and refrigerate while the EGG heats.
3. Melt butter in a large skillet and fry the egg s for 2 minutes on each side.
4. Preheat the EGG to 400°F.
5. Place bacon on a small cookie sheet and place on the grid in the EGG (R). Cook until crispy.
6. Place the patties on the grid and close the dome for 3 minutes.
7. Flip the burgers and replace the dome for an additional 3 minutes.
8. Close all of the vents and allow the burgers to sit for an additional 5 minutes. The internal temperature of the burger should be 150°F.
9. Place cheese on top of the burgers and cover for 1 more minute.
10. Assemble the burgers by placing a burger on the bottom bun, topping with bacon, tomato, and a fried egg .

Classic American Burger

Cook Time: 10-12 minutes
Servings: 4

Ingredients:

- 2 lbs ground beef
- 1/2 tsp salt
- 1/4 tsp pepper
- 4 slices American cheese
- 4 hamburger buns
- Green leaf lettuce
- Sliced tomato
- Ketchup
- Mustard
- Sliced pickle

Method:

1. Form ground beef into four patties and season both sides with salt and pepper.
2. Preheat the EGG to 500°F.
3. Place burgers on the grid and close the dome for 3 minutes.
4. Flip burgers and close the dome for 2 more minutes.
5. Close all of the vents and allow the burgers to sit for 5 minutes.
6. Top each burger with a slice of cheese and close the dome for 1 more minute.
7. Build burgers with lettuce, tomato, pickle, mustard, and ketchup.

Chicken Keema Burgers

Cook Time: 11-12 minutes

Servings: 4

Ingredients:

- 2 lbs ground chicken
- 1/2 cup fresh breadcrumbs
- 1 tablespoon olive oil
- 2 cloves garlic, finely chopped
- 1 small onion, finely chopped
- 1 egg
- 4 pieces naan
- 2 tablespoons Indian spice rub
- 1/2 cup Greek style yogurt
- 1/2 cup finely chopped, seeded, cucumber
- 2 tablespoons chopped fresh cilantro
- 1 tsp finely chopped green onion
- 1/4 tsp ground cumin

Method:

1. In a small bowl, combine ingredients for the raita and set aside. The raita can be made a day in advance, covered, and refrigerated.
2. In a small skillet, heat olive oil over medium and add onion and garlic. Cook until soft and translucent. Set aside to cool.
3. In a medium bowl, combine ground chicken, bread crumbs, onion mixture, egg, and Indian Spice Rub until combined. Form 4 patties and return to the fridge to chill for 10 minutes.
4. Preheat the EGG to 500°F.
5. Place burgers on the grid and close the dome for 3 minutes.
6. Flip burgers and close the dome for 3 more minutes.
7. Close all of the vents and allow the burgers to sit for 5-6 minutes or until the internal temperature reaches 170°F.
8. Serve burgers on naan, topped with raita.

The Crowned Jewels Burger

Cook Time: 10-12 minutes
Servings: 4

Ingredients:

- 2 lbs ground beef
- 1/2 tsp salt
- 1/4 tsp pepper
- 1 lb thinly sliced pastrami
- 1 cup shredded romaine lettuce
- 1/4 cup mayonnaise
- 2 tablespoons ketchup
- 1/8 tsp onion powder
- 4 slices sharp cheddar cheese
- 4 hamburger buns
- 1 tomato, sliced

Method:

1. Form ground beef into four patties and season both sides with salt and pepper.
2. Meanwhile, mix together mayonnaise, ketchup, and onion powder. Smear on each bun.
3. Place each pastrami and cheese covered burger on the prepared buns and top with shredded lettuce and tomato.
4. Preheat the EGG to 500°F.
5. Place burgers on the grid and close the dome for 3 minutes.
6. Flip burgers and close the dome for 2 more minutes.
7. Close all of the vents and allow the burgers to sit for 5 minutes.
8. Top each burger with 1/4 of the pastrami and a slice of cheese and close the dome for 1 more minute.

The Best Turkey Burger Ever

Cook Time: 10-12 minutes
Servings: 4

Ingredients:

- 1½ pounds ground turkey (a mixture of white and dark meat is best)
- 1/2 cup fresh breadcrumbs
- 1/4 cup shredded onion
- 1/4 cup shredded Granny Smith apple
- 1/2 tsp salt
- 1/4 tsp pepper
- 1 egg, beaten
- 1 clove garlic, grated
- 1/4 cup mayonnaise
- 2 tablespoon Besto Pesto
- 1/2 tsp sriracha
- 1 cup arugula
- 4 brioche buns
- 1 Granny Smith apple, thinly sliced

Method:

1. In a large bowl, combine burger ingredients well. Form into 4 patties and refrigerate while the EGG comes to temperature.
2. Preheat the EGG to 450°F.
3. Place turkey burgers onto the grid and close the dome for 3 minutes.
4. Flip the burgers and close the dome for another 3 minutes.
5. Close all of the vents and allow the burgers to sit for 5 minutes more or until the internal temperature reaches 170°F.
6. Stir together aioli mixture.
7. Remove the burgers and serve on a toasted brioche bun with arugula, thinly sliced apple, and a healthy smear of the aioli.

Oahu Burger

Cook Time: 10-12 minutes
Servings: 4

Ingredients:

- 2 lbs ground beef
- 1/4 cup thickened Teriyaki Marinade
- 1/4 cup mayonnaise
- 1/2 tsp sambal or sriracha
- 4 slices fresh pineapple, cored
- 4 slices tomato
- 4 slices butter lettuce
- 4 Hawaiian hamburger buns

Method:

1. Form ground beef into four patties and season both sides with salt and pepper.
2. In a small bowl, mix mayonnaise with hot chile sauce and spread on buns.
3. Top each bun with a burger, slice of pineapple, lettuce and tomato.
4. Preheat the EGG to 500°F.
5. Place burgers on the grid and close the dome for 3 minutes.
6. Flip burgers, baste with Teriyaki Marinade, and place the pineapple slices on the grid. Close the dome for 2 more minutes.
7. Flip the burgers again and baste with remaining Teriyaki Marinade. Close the dome.
8. Close all of the vents and allow the burgers to sit for 5 minutes.

"The Masterpiece"

Cook Time: 10-12 minutes
Servings: 4

Ingredients:

- 2 lbs ground beef
- 6 ounces sliced mushrooms
- 4 tablespoons shredded smoked gouda
- 2 tablespoons butter
- 2 tablespoons olive oil
- 2 tablespoons Dijon mustard
- 1/2 tsp salt
- 1/4 tsp pepper
- 8 slices bacon, cooked and crumbled
- 4 slices Swiss cheese
- 4 brioche buns
- 1 small onion, sliced

Method:

1. Heat a skillet over medium heat and add 1 Tablespoon butter and 1 Tablespoon olive oil.
2. Place mushrooms in the pan and DO NOT MOVE THEM. Saute for 5-7 minutes or until the mushrooms are browned. Remove from the pan and set aside.
3. In the same skillet, heat remaining butter and olive oil and add onions. Saute over medium heat until they become translucent and begin to brown, about 10 minutes. Remove from the heat and set aside to cool.
4. Mix onion, mushrooms, and crumbled bacon.
5. Preheat the EGG to 425°F.
6. Form ground beef into eight patties and season both sides with salt and pepper.
7. Place a generous spoonful of the mushroom and onion mixture in the center of four patties and top with smoked Gouda.
8. Top with additional patty and press sides to seal the mixture inside.
9. Place burgers on the grid and close the dome for 5 minutes.
10. Flip burgers and close the dome for 3 more minutes.
11. Close all of the vents and allow the burgers to sit for 5 minutes.
12. Top each burger with a slice of Swiss cheese and close the dome for 1 more minute.
13. Spread buns with mustard, top with burgers and bun tops.

Ham And Cheese Panini

Cook Time: 15 minutes

Servings: 4

Ingredients:

- 4 slices of Parma ham
- Deli-smoked ham -1/2 pound
- Spicy brown mustard -1/4 cup
- 8 slices whole wheat bread
- 8 slices sharp white Cheddar cheese
- Packed baby arugula -2 cups
- 1 ripe Bartlett pear, cored and cut into 20 thin slices
- Olive oil

Method:

1. Evenly spread the mustard over one side of each slice of bread.
2. Top each of the 4 slices of bread with 1 slice of cheese along with half of the arugula.
3. Add the slices of pear and ham and top with the remaining arugula, Cheddar cheese, and slices of bread.
4. Press the sandwiches together. Lightly brush the outside of the sandwiches with oil.
5. Cook the sandwiches on the griddle, flipping over once, until the cheese entirely melts, and the bread is golden.

Chapter 11: Rubs, Marinades, and Sauces

Classic American Brown Sugar Rub

Ingredients:

- 1/2 cup light brown sugar
- 1/4 c smoked paprika
- 4 tablespoons kosher salt
- 3 tablespoons black pepper
- 2 tsp onion powder
- 2 tsp garlic powder
- 2 tsp celery seed
- 1 tsp red pepper flakes

Method:

1. Combine ingredients in a small bowl.
2. Rub onto meat and skin and allow to sit at least 30 minutes before smoking or grilling.
3. Unused portions can be kept in an airtight container for up to 6 months.

English Pub Rub

Ingredients:

- 1 beef bouillon cube, pulverized
- 2 cloves garlic, crushed
- 1 small shallot, finely diced
- 1 tsp kosher salt
- 1/4 c extra-virgin olive oil

Method:

1. Combine ingredients in a small bowl and slather on the steaks.
2. Allow to sit at least 30 minutes before smoking.

Berbere Spice Mix

Ingredients:

- 1 tablespoon paprika
- 1½ tsp cayenne pepper
- 1½ tsp ground ginger
- 1 tsp ground allspice
- 1 tsp ground cumin
- 1/2 tsp nutmeg
- 1/2 tsp ground cinnamon
- 1/2 tsp dried oregano
- 1/4 tsp ground cloves

Method:

1. Combine ingredients in a small bowl.
2. Rub onto meat and skin and allow to sit at least one hour before smoking.
3. Unused portions can be kept in an airtight container for up to 6 months.

Asian Rub

Ingredients:

- 1/4 c paprika (Spanish or sweet paprika works best)
- 2 tablespoons dry mustard
- 2 tablespoons Chinese five spice powder
- 2 tablespoons ground ginger
- 1 tablespoon salt
- 1 tablespoon pepper
- 1 tablespoon crushed red pepper flakes

Method:

1. Combine all ingredients in a small bowl.
2. May be stored in an airtight container for up to 6 months.

Adobo Rub

Ingredients:

- 1 tablespoon ancho chili powder
- 1 teaspoon ground cumin
- 1 tsp onion powder
- 1 tsp garlic powder
- 1 tsp salt
- 1/2 tsp pepper
- The juice of 1 lime
- 2 Tablespoons extra-virgin olive oil

Method:

1. Thoroughly combine ingredients in a small bowl and rub on chicken or pork.
2. Allow to sit for 4-6 hours or overnight before smoking.

Habanero Rub

Ingredients:

- 3 tablespoons onion powder
- 2 tablespoons garlic powder
- 2 tablespoons paprika
- 2 tablespoons light brown sugar
- 1 tablespoon ground allspice
- 1 tablespoon ground chipotle chile powder
- 2 tsp ground cinnamon
- 2 tsp ground thyme
- 1 tsp ground habanero chile powder
- 1 tsp ground dried lemon peel
- 1/2 tsp ground nutmeg

Method:

1. Combine ingredients in a small bowl.
2. Rub onto meat and skin and allow to sit at least one hour before smoking.
3. Unused portions can be kept in an airtight container for up to 6 months.
4. Tip: You can find habanero chile powder online, but if you are in a pinch, substitute cayenne pepper and increase the dried lemon peel to 1½ tsp.

Chile Rub

Ingredients:

- 4 dried New Mexico chiles
- 4 dried guajillo chiles
- 4 dried ancho chiles
- 1/2 c cumin seeds
- 1/4 c dried oregano
- 1/4 c paprika
- 3 tablespoons kosher salt
- 1 tablespoon onion powder
- 2 tsp garlic powder

Method:

1. Combine all ingredients into a spice grinder and pulse until thoroughly ground.
2. Then add onion powder and garlic powder.
3. Combine ingredients in a small bowl.
4. Rub onto meat and skin and allow to sit at least one hour before smoking.
5. Unused portions can be kept in an airtight container for up to 6 months.

Carne Asada Rub

Ingredients:

- 2 cloves garlic, crushed
- 2 tablespoons lime juice
- 2 tablespoons orange juice
- 2 tablespoons extra-virgin olive oil
- 1 tablespoon lime zest
- 1 tablespoon orange zest
- 1 tsp ancho chili powder
- 1 tsp cumin
- 1 tsp salt
- 1/2 tsp pepper
- 1/2 tsp Mexican oregano

Method:

1. Combine in a small bowl.
2. Slather on the meat and allow it to sit at least 30 minutes before smoking or grilling.

Country Style Rub

Ingredients:

- 1 cup white sugar
- 1/2 c kosher salt
- 1/4 c sweet paprika
- 2 tablespoons garlic powder
- 1 tablespoon ground cumin
- 1 tablespoon cayenne pepper
- 1 tablespoon black pepper
- 1 tsp ground celery seed

Method:

1. Combine ingredients in a small bowl.
2. Rub onto meat and skin and allow to sit at least one hour before smoking.
3. Unused portions can be kept in an airtight container for up to 6 months.

Mediterranean Spice Rub

Ingredients:

- 3 tablespoons dried rosemary
- 2 tablespoons ground cumin
- 2 tablespoons ground coriander
- 1 tablespoon dried oregano
- 2 tsp ground cinnamon
- 2 tsp garlic powder
- 1 tsp kosher salt

Method:

1. Combine ingredients in a small bowl.
2. Rub onto meat and skin and allow to sit at least one hour before smoking.
3. Unused portions can be kept in an airtight container for up to 6 months.

Chapter 12: Game

Venison fillets

Cook Time: 35 minutes
Servings: 6

Ingredients:

- 1 venison fillet, skinned and cut into 6 equal portions (3-lbs, 1.36-kgs)
- Sea salt and freshly ground black pepper

Method:

1. Place the 6 fillets on the grid, season with salt and black pepper, and close the EGG'S lid. Give the venison a quarter turn after 2 minutes and once again, close the lid.
2. After 2 minutes, flip the venison over and repeat until you see charred marks on both sides of the meat.
3. Remove the venison from the EGG and loosely tent with foil.
4. Allow the meat to rest for 5 minutes, before cutting.
5. Serve and enjoy.

Saddle Of Hare With Parsnips, Cabbage, And Apple

Cook Time: 1 hours
Servings: 4

Ingredients:

- 2 saddles of hare, membranes removed
- 4 tbsp olive oil
- 1 onion, peeled and finely chopped
- 3 parsnips, peeled and cut into cubes
- 3 Granny Smith apples, cored and cut into cubes
- 1 red cabbage, cut into strips
- Water -1¾ cups
- Sea salt and black pepper

Method:

1. Place a skillet on the grid, add the oil and heat.
2. Add the onion to the hot oil and fry for a couple of minutes.
3. Next, add the parsnip along with the apple and fry for an additional 1-2 minutes.
4. Stir in the cabbage and fry for an additional 2 minutes, while occasionally turning the vegg ies. Close the EGG 'S lid after every action.
5. Deglaze the vegg ies with the water, stir and season with salt and pepper.
6. Remove the skillet from the grid.
7. Place the hare saddles directly on the grid and grill for 2 minutes. Turn them over and grill for an additional 2 minutes.
8. Rest the saddles of hare, meat side facing upward on the vegg ies in the skillet.
9. Place the skillet on the center of the grid.
10. Insert a meat thermometer into the center of one of the hare saddles. Set the core temperature to 125°F (52°C) and close the EGG 'S lid.
11. Cook for 20 minutes, or until the meat's core temperature is achieved.
12. Remove the skillet from the EGG and using the back of a spoon, fillet the hare.
13. Season with sea salt and pepper and serve with the braised red cabbage and apples.

Asian-Style Wild Boar Ribs

Cook Time: 5 hours 45 minutes
Servings: 4

Ingredients:

- Wild boar ribs, cut into 1 rib portions (6-lbs, 2.7-kgs)
- Soy sauce -3/4 cup
- Dry sherry -2/3 cup
- Packed dark brown sugar -1/2 cup
- 6 garlic cloves, peeled and minced
- Cayenne pepper -1 tablespoon
- Fresh ginger, grated -1 tablespoon
- Chinese 5-spice powder -2 teaspoons

Method:

1. Trim the ribs of any excess fat and in a single layer arrange the ribs in a drip pan.
2. Next, prepare the marinade: In a pan, combine the soy sauce with the dry sherry, dark brown sugar, garlic, cayenne pepper, ginger, and Chinese 5-spice powder.
3. Cook over moderate heat until the sugar entirely dissolves.
4. Remove the pan from the heat and allow to slightly cool.
5. Pour the marinade over the ribs.
6. Cover and transfer to the fridge for 60 minutes, flipping the ribs over once.
7. Cover the drip pan with aluminum foil.
8. Place the drip pan on the grid and cook for 45 minutes.
9. Remove the ribs from the pan and place on the grid.
10. Cook for an additional 45-60 minutes until the ribs are tender, while occasionally brushing with the marinade.
11. Brush the brush once again with the marinade and serve.

Conclusion

The ultimate how-to guide your big green egg smoker, use this complete guide to smoke all types of meat, seafood, game and veggies. An essential cookbook for those who want to smoke meat without needing expert help from others. Offers detailed guidance obtained by years of smoking meat includes clear instructions and step-by-step directions for every recipe.

The Unofficial Big Green Egg Cookbook includes temperature charts, helpful tips and tricks on making BBQ and SMOKING MEAT to make your job easier. Whether you are a beginner meat smoker or looking to go beyond the basics, the book gives you the tools and tips you need to start that perfectly smoked meat.

www.ingramcontent.com/pod-product-compliance
Lightning Source LLC
Chambersburg PA
CBHW081402070526
44583CB00020B/2636